CARAVANSARY
and
CONVERSATION

Memories of
Places and Persons

CARAVANSARY
and
CONVERSATION

Memories of
Places and Persons

By
RICHARD CURLE

. . . . and combined the information.
—*Dickens*

Essay Index Reprint Series

BOOKS FOR LIBRARIES PRESS
FREEPORT, NEW YORK

INTERNATIONAL STANDARD BOOK NUMBER:
0-8369-2151-8

LIBRARY OF CONGRESS CATALOG CARD NUMBER:
73-134070

PRINTED IN THE UNITED STATES OF AMERICA

To

JIM AND CALVERT OSBORNE,

MY VIRGINIA "COUSINS"

Contents

CONTENTS

Introduction

THE TITLE OF THIS
book, though rather fanciful, gives a clear enough hint
of its range. "Caravansary" stands for travel and "Conversation" for people. My general plan has been to
alternate chapters on places with chapters on persons,
and thus achieve a certain variety. And I have tried to
link the chapters together by little prefaces at the head
of each and so give some homogeneity to a work which,
from its contents-table, might appear very disconnected.

In former years I wrote two other volumes of travel,
Wanderings and *Into the East*, and in a sense, this book,
in so far as it fills up gaps, may be said to supplement
them. The three together yield a fairly complete picture
of my journeys throughout the world, and if, in the
travel parts of the present volume, I have devoted myself, in the main, to but a few countries, the reason is that
I have more or less exhausted my material. Even so,
however, these pages do touch upon five continents.

So far as travel is concerned, the underlying idea of

Caravansary and Conversation is, as in my other travel books, to create atmosphere. That seems to me the important thing in a work of this nature. And as for my reminiscences of famous characters, they may be called sketches in a more or less impressionistic manner: sometimes by an economy of words one gets the happiest effects in evoking personality. In both instances I can only hope that I have succeeded in doing what I have endeavoured to do.

R. C.

Fez, the Unchanging

▽

This recollection of Fez dates back about a dozen years. I am sure that the outward appearance of the city is virtually the same now as it was then—the nature of its construction forbids any drastic attempt at modernizing; but as for other matters, well, "all passes and all changes." I have not attempted any revision of facts. That would be beyond me. I only want to recall what things were like in those uneasy days when Abd-el-Krim was still menacing the French from the fastnesses of the Riff.

CHAPTER I

Fez, the Unchanging

STARTING FROM RABAT, ON
the Atlantic, after a not too early breakfast, we reached
Fez before the first coolness of the afternoon. And in
that short sentence is epitomized the French mastery
over central Morocco, where there is no longer turbu-
lence but peace and where perfectly engineered roads
have taken the place of weary desert tracks. From the
city of the Sultan and the Resident-General we passed
through the great cork forest beyond, out into the withered bled, dotted by the low black tents of the nomadic
Moors of the plain, and so to Meknes, with its massive
ruins and its memories of that uncouth and pitiless imi-
tator of Louis XIV, Mulai Ismail.

A couple of hours' run from Meknes brought us to
Fez. The sun poured upon the car, and tired, hot and
dusty, I would have made straight for our hotel, but my
friend, who knew what was in store for me in the first
sight of the city, would not let us descend until he had

3

shown me the panorama from the hill beyond. Skirting the Jewish quarter—new Fez, Fez-jedid—we climbed the ridge.

"Don't look down till we stop," said he, making for a special point. "Now," he added, slowing up, "look! There is Fez."

Yes, there was Fez. It lay before us—old Fez, Fez-el-Bali—basking beneath its sandy hills, mounting towards the west, surrounded by its crenellated, crumbling brown walls and its gardens of olive and cypress. Near and far green-tiled minarets pierced beyond the dove-coloured flat roofs, and the whole town, clustered beneath us in its silence and its peace, was like some rich vision of the Orient come to appease the traveller in this stony land.

The shape of Fez is roughly that of a figure eight: Fez-el-Bali narrows to a neck at its highest point and beyond that neck spreads Fez-jedid, the mellah or home of the Jews, which in all its eight hundred years of existence has never achieved an internal dignity or character, but whose outer line of houses, tall, ancient and uneven, has a picturesqueness of its own, as from this vantage-ground it disappears into the level, past the summit of old Fez.

Over the shoulder of the opposite hill the outline of the Middle Atlas undulates in a mauve curve, and to the east, Fez-el-Bali, cut short by its encompassing wall, is fronted by a mass of deep green herbage, fading into a burnt savanna that will soon blossom once more.

Altogether, a noble and moving sight, and one full, as it were, of the genius of Arabia. Not Damascus, not Baghdad, not Mecca itself, I venture to think, could hold the spirit of the Mohammedan world with a more soothing harmony of completeness. Even to gaze down upon Fez is to feel transported; its associations, its whole appearance, arouse in one the sense of living, aged history.

I looked long upon the city, as if my eyes could never be done with feasting on its beauty and drinking from that well of pure delight. But it was even more enthralling when, just before the September sunset, we clambered to the top of the Dar Jamai, a palace of the lower town, once the home of a Grand Vizier, and saw Fez-el-Bali crouching at our very feet. The heat of the day had gone, and the noises of the town, carried up to us in a confused murmur from the deep and narrow streets, vibrated about us in the sunset air.

And presently from that high terrace we beheld a sight which no male eyes should look upon: on to the roofs of Fez gaily dressed women, now singly, now in groups, began to emerge, vivacious, waving to one another, gathering in eager clusters, wives, daughters, slave-girls happy together, until it was almost as if above the hidden streets of men another world of women had risen, unsuspected.

In the unrehearsed spontaneity of the scene, the

5

cloistered women of Fez, freed from the restraints of the Moslem code and safe from the jealous, prying eyes of their menfolk, had thrown aside altogether the demure severity of their manner and were enjoying the fine evening like children released from the pose of playing a part in company. Flocks of pigeons and egrets flew over the cypress groves and swifts circled the tower on which we stood. The level beams of the sunset fell ever more softly upon old Fez, the women reluctantly began to descend from the roofs to greet their lords, and a breath of the coming night trembled in the branches of the orange trees in the Vizier's garden.

Idyllic?—Well, I am not so sure. In that atmosphere of the East, in the whole walled pageant of the town, there was the suggestion of something sinister and secretive, the hint of things hidden for ever from the light of day. The concealed loveliness of palace and courtyard—for all that is lovely and calm in Fez is hidden and tucked away—seemed in itself a form of corruption, as though it fostered within its beauty a voluptuous debasement.

This is, I dare say, a fanciful interpretation, for the European delights in sensing the cruel splendour of the East, but all the same I believe that no one could have stared down upon Fez from that balcony without being conscious of its profoundly alien civilization. It holds for one's thought the very essence of Arabia's arid and fanatic heart.

And then suddenly from one of the central mosques the white flag of the Prophet was run up on the masthead and instantaneously, as if but waiting for the lead, it fluttered here and there over the town, while the muezzins, appearing at each corner of their minarets in turn, robed figures against the sky, called upon Believers to assemble and pray. Their high-pitched voices, trained to carry, blended into a marvellous drone above the city, and from far across the town came the thin, clear notes, like an echo of the nearer ones, rising, dying away—the very accents of an enduring faith.

Of the five daily calls to prayer, the evening call sounds most appealing to the stranger, so romantic is the setting of twilight above an Eastern city. The end of the hot day's toil, the praise before the darkness of the night. Mohammed certainly had an eye to effect, and often as one may hear that call, one cannot hear it ever without being touched.

From the hotel near the entrance to the mellah, one dives sharply down into Fez-el-Bali. And in an instant, without a guide, one would be utterly lost in the teeming warren of its tortuous labyrinths. This is a literal truth, and Europeans have assured me that it requires months to know one's way about Fez. The main streets are only lanes, perhaps twelve feet wide, and the side streets but slits of darkness between dead walls. They radiate and cross and multiply, always alike in their differences, always bewildering; they disappear down dim steps and under arches; they resemble a maze, full of the noise of bargaining and the shuffle of feet or hushed in the muffled silence of the Orient. Laden donkeys are driven in with firewood and grain from the country, shopkeepers sit in cross-legged rows in their cubbyholes a few feet above the ground, a great man passes in disdainful aloofness upon his red-caparisoned mule, women sidle along, swathed from head to foot, children play, blind men are led by little boys, beggars monotonously crave alms in the name of a saint, Moors and Negroes and Berbers—hardly a Jew, in his black jalouba and cap, is to be seen in Fez-el-Bali, the one centre in Morocco where business is forbidden to the Israelite—brush shoulders with one another in the throng.

The babel of this intensive life fills all the day, and yet there is none of what one might call the concerted noise of the Western world. Each man goes about his business wrapped in an impenetrable inner silence. An old lawyer crouches in an alcove listening to a client, aloof from the crowd as if in the privacy of an office; a tradesman fingers his amber beads, lost to mundane things; a Negro slave stands vacantly at a corner awaiting his master; and people in general regard not one another, intent upon their own affairs.

The Oued Fez, flowing down through the city by

8

innumerable underground channels, can be glimpsed occasionally as it dashes out of a culvert to drive a water wheel or heard as it gurgles in some hidden rill beyond a wall. The sound of running water is never far away. And all over the city the exquisite mosaic fountains, unchanged in design throughout the centuries, bear witness to its blessings; though having observed the grey, polluted colour of the stream, I was not in the least surprised to learn that typhoid is an annual epidemic. Mohammedans take no precautions: Allah is the arbiter of men's lives and fate cannot be evaded.

In the centre of the town, where the different trades, dyers, tile workers, cloth and leather merchants, weavers, and so forth, have their separate quarters, the houses are low and the streets are shaded from the sun by plaited grass stretched from roof to roof. The light strikes through in splashes and the effect is like walking beneath a pergola, though the smells are scarcely such as we associate with rural scenes. But elsewhere, as I have suggested, the streets resemble gashes between high, blank walls, whose only signs of life are iron-studded doors and occasional barred windows. The Easterner, both from natural habit and from long experience that ostentatious wealth is liable to end badly, prefers to hide his luxurious tastes from the public eye. The palaces of the rich are reached through cramped, black passages that might open on to a hovel rather than a marble courtyard. The merchant, leaving his

9

mansion in the morning, emerges with sedate humility, dressed in simple white burnous like his fellow-men, and is no longer the wealthy head of a family but the struggling Believer. He does not advertise his prosperity; rather does he seek to create the impression that the world is a hard place and that only by pious exercises and attention to business can a poor man hope to succeed.

But hospitality being enjoined upon the Arabs, when one is invited to a feast all is different and the proper thing in a host is to display his consequence. I have had a variety of meals in Fez houses, but the description of a typical dinner will suffice for all. The one I have in mind was partaken of with a man who lived at the very other end of Fez from where we were staying, and I will not readily forget that walk through the darkened, sleeping city. He had sent a Negro slave to show us the way, and that simple old man, first kissing our hands in token of his devotion, led on with a lamp through the windings of the silent town. The sense of a thousand years of changeless history hung upon the air; the death-like quiet, the furtive prowling figures, the watchmen resting at the different gates—the city is divided up into sections, shut off from one another at night—, the queer Oriental feeling of being observed by unseen eyes, the odorous, veiled and stifling night— all this was as the prelude to an adventure of the Golden Age.

And then, at last, the door in the wall, the knocks, the slave crouching within, the opened portal, the flood of light from the brilliant courtyard with its marble fountain spilling over into a basin, and the figure of our host stepping forward, suave, inscrutable, in fine-spun robes, welcoming us to his home, courteously introducing us to the members of his family designated to share with us the honour of the banquet.

Moorish domestic architecture, like everything that has come out of Arabia, has long since achieved its final form, and the design of one great house in Fez is, in essentials, the design of all. In a city like Marrakesh, with its African influence, and in the strongholds of the Atlas chieftains, the Arabian impress has been modified, but Fez is a purely Eastern city in all but name. The paved courtyard is open to the sky—powdered on these clear autumn nights with points of fire like gold-dust scattered upon a velvet curtain—and the pillars around, supporting the arches of the recesses, are inlaid elaborately with tiles of different colours, while the fretwork and tracery of the stucco porticoes and cedar roofs are intricately carved in Saracenic patterns. Rich men expend vast sums on the elaboration of such ornament, and the whole effect is one of severe magnificence.

In the upper storey the apartments of the women surround the court, and their shadowy forms are visible, now and then, as they peep down curiously at the guests; but below, the house is solely for the use of the men. The rooms, alas, are only too tawdrily furnished. They contain nothing of the antique—I doubt whether there is one ancient manuscript in the whole of Fez—, no old carpets, illuminated Korans or beaten metal, but only vulgar ornaments, garish German clocks, divans covered with crude stuffs and bedsteads all brass and glitter. I do not know why it is, but a Fez merchant yearns to show his prosperity by the number of clocks, none of which seem to be going, he can squeeze into one room, and by the gorgeousness of his bedsteads, none of which ever seem to be slept in; yet it is no exaggeration to say that these two articles of furniture are the visible signs of financial stability.

The house we were dining at that night belonged to an oil merchant, an owner of farms outside the boundaries and a man of substance. We had begged him not to provide too sumptuous a meal, so there were but five courses in all, heralded by those three tumblers of mint tea which compose the proper accompaniment of every Moorish repast. When we were ushered into the dwelling room, which was merely one of the recesses off the courtyard, we all sat down in a row upon a divan, while our host seated himself opposite and kept up, through the interpreter, a polite trickle of complimentary talk. With his fair beard and complexion he may well have claimed descent from the Andalusian Moors and it is hard to say what nationality one would have given him in European dress. His face was pensive in repose, and the faint, puzzled smile that momentarily passed over his features had something dreamy and abstracted about it, as if, present in body, he was absent in spirit.

Soon he slipped away to superintend the serving of the dinner—it is one of the embarrassing adjuncts of such meals that the host seldom sits down with you, but hovers around, anxious and alert, marshalling the servants and seeing that all is well—and his place was taken by his brother, to whom fell the task, honourable indeed, of making tea.

And now, behold, a band of musicians had seated themselves in the courtyard and, starting without more ado, played incessantly for several hours. And ever and again one or another of them would lift up his voice in song, throwing his head into the air like a howling dog and emitting sounds as barbaric and meaningless to our ears as those of the accompanying music. But it was a marked compliment to pay and we endured it all with becoming unconcern.

The making of tea is a rite of long usage and definite routine. A plated silver urn is put before the maker, together with sugar, mint, tea, and a number of small glass tumblers. It is always green tea that is served, the taste for which was acquired many years ago through the Moorish pirates capturing a cargo of it in the Mediterranean. The fresh mint is crammed into a receptacle at the top of the urn and the boiling water is poured over it, while the sugar, in lumps half as big as one's fist, is dropped in in such quantities that the resulting concoction is almost like a syrup. And yet it is not disagreeable, though it cloys.

And so, when the tea is cleared away, the slave girls, dark Negresses or fairest of Berbers but usually comely and contemptuous, hand round from guest to guest a basin of metal, into which they pour water over your outstretched palms. The divans are gathered into a semi-circle: in the midst is a low, round table, resembling a "dumb-waiter," on which the courses are placed in a succession of gigantic, steaming dishes. For each guest a napkin, a loaf of flat bread, and the power to use the thumb and first two fingers of his right hand. Course after course comes on and disappears, first to the wives, then to the slaves: eggs floating in melted butter, thick with shredded onions; mutton seasoned and stewed in a rich gravy; pigeons roasted whole; chickens stuffed with almonds; a high-piled kus-kus, its semolina savoury with scraps of meat (the almost invariable finale), until one hardly knows how to get through and scarce can swallow the tit-bits pressed specially upon one by the host. There is nothing to drink but water, which it is inadvisable to drink, and by the end of the meal one's napkin, mouth, fingers and probably one's clothes are in a state of odious messiness. And then the ablutions once more, words of effusive thanks, a short, strained wait, and—the dark streets and homeward trudge.

The Moor conducts his hospitality with grave countenance, but Moors differ, like other people, and a few
are almost uproarious in their sense of fun. I recollect
once lunching at a house in Fez where many Cadis
were assembled to do honour to a new Cadi of the district, a most likeable, lively man. Occasionally, forget-
ting what I was doing, I would feed myself with my
left hand, only to remember suddenly and withdraw it
in guilty haste, and that old Cadi opposite would rock
with laughter. He asked through the interpreter
whether I had ever been to Arabia; in answer to which
I drew my hand across my throat. Whereat he bade
him tell me in the most expansive good humour that I
could safely venture within ten miles of Mecca—and he
a Cadi, interpreter of the Sacred Law!

Mohammedans, petrified long since by the tenets of
the Koran, which govern their outlook upon the universe and order their lives, are peculiarly subject to
minute observances. Their irresponsive minds, unable
to expand in modern channels, find solace in a strict
carrying out of all the commands of their founder. If
they are charitable and compassionate, if they are hospitable and courteous, it is largely because they have
been instructed so to be. I do not mean that they are
devoid of natural feelings, but that their good qualities,
like their bad, are enhanced and made rigid by the
teachings of their creed. Their piety is fanatic rather
than personal, their charity is a claim on paradise, their

views on women and education and science have never really altered since about the Thirteenth Century, when the last great commentator on the Koran exhausted its adaptability to the problems of the day.

Fez, one of the chief centres of Arabian learning, is frozen in its mediæval ideas. Its heart has altered no more than its face, and that is what makes it for the passer-by a city of romance and of incredible strangeness. Its medersa or universities, lovely in their mellow age—they must be six to eight hundred years old—are crumbling away, and only here and there have the French insisted on the stucco work and the tiles being renewed. But that is the fatalism of the East; everything decays and yet everything goes on unchanged. Tolba (students) still crowd the medersa, living in dirty little rooms in the upper storeys, washing by the courtyard fountain, listening year after year to the antiquated teaching of men learned and devout, absorbing the philosophy of the Koran, studying the hair-splitting commentators, fortifying themselves in faith and fanaticism.

I have been over several of these medersa, though I have never been inside the Kairouan, which is mosque and university combined and, apart from the El-Ajhar in Cairo, the largest seat of Moslem education in North Africa and, I presume, the world. No Unbeliever can enter there, but from the roof of the Attarin school near by I have seen into its sacred courtyard and gazed upon this hidden place made bare.

The Attarin stands within the area of low streets in the medina or centre of the town, and from its roof one hears a noise as of a hive of bees, a ceaseless hum, borne upwards from the invisible suks. Near and far rise the minarets of famous mosques, Kairouan, Mulai Idris, Andalusia, Boushaniyar, Sidi Khazim-el-Tizane, Bab Guissa, and many others—Fez has twenty-two chief mosques and four hundred lesser ones—, gleaming green or white in the sun that beats so fiercely upon everything; and about you the town, on its upward slope towards Fez-jedid, on its decline in the east towards the gardens of the outskirts, gives you a complete central picture of this queer conglomeration of intersected roofs.

Under the arched bridges of the lower town, to the south, the remnant of the dirty river flows, and beyond that the streets twist about the yards of the stone-masons. Looking down upon all, upon the massed buildings of this Oriental scene, one cannot but feel in one's bones the static civilization of Arabia. This city full of secrets, of a licentious sterility of imagination, lies, so to speak, within the hollow of your hand, and all its hot, Eastern breath floats about you.

And as one wanders through the streets day after day, deeper and deeper sinks in the personality of the place. No Unbeliever is allowed to pass the threshold of any mosque in Morocco, and such a one cannot even ap-

proach the precincts of so holy a spot as the Mulai Idris
(so called from the founder of the city), whose horm, or
sacred influence, stretches out into the adjacent alley-
ways and is marked off by wooden barriers across the
streets. And if impossible to penetrate into a mosque,
it is unwise to linger by the entrance, though, as one
passes, one may glance casually in and observe the
white-robed worshippers and see perhaps—incongruous
climax—a row of grandfather clocks bequeathed by
some pious patron. Outside, people, poor women for
the most part, offer bowed supplications through the
gratings in the wall, tying coloured threads to the iron
bars; beggars, horribly maimed and diseased, sit in list-
less rows; and miscellaneous bartering goes on with
particular fervour. And always fanaticism lies near the
surface, a fanaticism the more savage and incalculable in
that the pristine Mohammedanism of Arabia is overlaid
in Morocco by African fetishism and extravagance. In
the precincts of a mosque I have been faced by an old
man with red, blazing eyes and minatory gesture, a
Moslem impressive in the utter finality of his convictions. Indeed, under the calm, indifferent surface of
Fez one never ceases to be aware of something suppressed and dark in the passions of the mob.

The shops of this city are a sheer delight in their
Oriental quaintness. In that cellar-like kennel a baker
is baking the bread brought to him by his clients; here,
half filling the narrow lane, are tubs of vegetable dye,

and the dyers at their work are like dripping demons; and look at these fruit stalls, leather shops, piles of blue Fez pottery, heaps of sticky sweetmeats. They are precisely what one would have expected to see in such a city, they fit the mental picture, and consequently they satisfy. And sometimes, on your strolls, you will hear the plaint of many childish voices and, peering through a half-open door, you will see a little school at its lessons, the teacher reading from the Koran, his pupils squatting on the floor about him, intoning the words in unison, looking straight in front of them as if mesmerised—and that, too, is typical and thus delightful.

The most valuable import trade of Fez is cotton piece-goods, and this trade with England has flourished now for the better part of a century. There are firms here who have their own Moorish representative in Manchester and who do a yearly turnover of five hundred thousand pounds, for Fez is the distributing centre for the whole country. According to the Capitulations any firm whose trade with England is of an annual value of ten thousand pounds or more, is entitled, from year to year, to appoint one of its members to be under the protection of Great Britain. It was a privilege formerly of inestimable worth, when wealth aroused so readily the cupidity of Sultans and Pashas and when the means of satisfying it were so drastic and so simple. Now that the French are in nominal charge the privilege has no longer the same significance, but nevertheless it is prized, and the British Vice-Consul, with his judicial powers, has much to do, while the British post-office—where letters are not subject to the illicit investigation of the Arabs—makes a handsome profit.

We must remember that the policy of the French is to interfere as little as possible with internal administration and local customs. Certainly they do not allow prisoners to starve to death nowadays and certainly they do not permit those raids upon the mellah which used to replenish, every decade or so, the Arab purse and level up the balance between Moor and Jew; but slavery still exists. (Again, I am talking of 1924.) Theoretically, it is a thing of the past and, in actual fact, any slave can gain his freedom if he knows or cares how to go about it, but there is still a slave-market in Fez—it lies just below the palace of the Dar Jamai—and there are still many slaves. But their treatment is not bad, for the Koran is explicit on the point. They feed on the same food as their masters, they are housed and warmed, and their lives, I should suppose, are not unhappy within the limited range of their desires. To free a slave is to leave him penniless in a country where poverty is not a recommendation. So do not let our repulsion at the idea mislead us as to the actual practise.

As to the women slaves who wait upon one at table and are about the only women ever seen unveiled by a male stranger, the haughty indifference of their manner and their prepossessing appearance suggest that their position in the household, while perhaps invidious, is not by any means one of subjection. In fact, the wives and the slave girls live together practically as equals and cringing servility is quite unknown.

One hears much about the inferior standing occupied by Moslem women, but they exercise great, if imponderable, influence and are very far from being mere chattels. It is true that a Fez husband could, and probably would, kill an unfaithful wife without any questions being asked; but on the other hand, her status as regards property is secure and she is a person of importance. Most marriages are in the nature of a family alliance and the average husband is careful to treat his wives with that kindness Moorish wives expect: they have no wish to alienate useful friends. Companionship is neither given nor sought; the Moor is not an Occidental.

And as to being cooped up all day and fearfully bored, let us note, first, that Moorish women have few aims and interests in life, and, second, that certain of them do not lead so very cloistered an existence. When the husband goes forth in the morning he locks up his house with a preposterous key, a real Blue Beard's key, which hangs at his girdle and is, for all the world, symbolic of his masculine dominance; but the wife who wants to indulge in an escapade has only to skip over the roofs or concert a plan with some old hag, who acts as a go-between. One hears that this sort of thing is not uncommon, and though it is a dangerous game to play, whoever heard of danger curing the spirit of adventure? Strategy is the universal weapon against force.

The leather-work of Fez has an international reputation and, if much of it be trashy, much of it is graceful. But it is desirable to have somebody who knows the ropes to take one to where the finest specimens are obtainable. I had that luck—there are just a half-dozen Englishmen to whom Fez is, up to a point, an open book—and thus I was enabled to spend two mornings in the tiny shop of the foremost purveyor of Fez leather. I need not describe my purchases, but the man from whom I bought them I will describe. He was elderly, stout, and as he squatted in the depths of his shop with the shutters carefully closed, his crafty eyes ranged over us and he made whimpering exclamations of delight, like a startled little animal, while each treasure was unwrapped and laid before us. With sage noddings of the head as he listened to our desires, dramatic gestures of despair as we counter-offered, and a sigh of surrender as, after Arabic calculations, he accepted our price, he presented a real picture of the bargaining East. In front of him stood a glass bowl filled with the fresh petals of some flower and near by a bottle of pungent scent. The petals were pressed into our hands, the scent upon our handkerchiefs, and forthwith he proceeded to tie up the parcels with so extraordinary an intricacy of string-design that I wonder to this day whether it were not some cabalistic means of warding off the contamination of the Infidels. Or was it to prevent making a cross, which the normal tying of a package does make? At any rate, he seemed fairly contented, although his wails were ringing in our ears as we left him to count up his profits.

One of the exciting facts about Fez is that any doorway may lead to an Oriental picture which is exactly what you might read about in an old Arabian tale. I have mentioned the slave-market, seen by me through an open door, and I would mention now the lunatic asylum, whose unfortunate inmates are still, I was told (1924), chained to one another by yokes around their necks, an endless chain that passes through holes in the wall from cell to cell, and the Pasha's court, reached through an untidy, reeking passage, where justice is dealt out according to the precepts of the Orient.

The Pasha of Fez is the glorified Mayor of the town. That is to say, his mayoral powers approximate to those of a dictator. He is, of course, under the supervision of the French and must walk warily, but the French, as I have said, are loath to interfere with domestic jurisdiction. He is the judge, too, and sits cross-legged for many hours a day in an open recess at the upper end of the sunny courtyard, administering justice. He has power in all matters save those concerning land, women and religion, which fall within the province of the Cadi.

We rested beneath the shelter of a tree and watched

23

him. Rotund, white-bearded and impassive, he slowly and unceasingly fanned himself, while criminals trembled before him at the unfolded tale or litigants screamed at one another in simulated indignation. By his side sat a French assessor, at right angles crouched the scribes. In one sense of the word there is no formality in a Moorish court. The old mokhazni or Government servant (they are recognised by their peaked red caps) who stands always before him, chief usher of the court, appears to beckon forward whoever is nearest, and the civil and criminal cases follow one another indiscriminately. Now it is a peasant who has transgressed a by-law; now it is two men who wish him to arbitrate between them and will go away together, perfectly satisfied; now it is a thief who will be led to prison or some humble being who will be rewarded; now it is a rich man who can afford to bring a lawyer with him, fussily talkative and carrying an ostentatious satchel bulging with papers. The cases last but a few minutes on an average. In calm words the decision is announced: the dispute is settled, the wrong-doer is bastinadoed on the spot, the litigant is sent off to the Mosque to be sworn; judgment, in short, in any of its different varieties, is given without waste of time. The Pasha is a member of the old school, stern for the ancient usages, devoid of pity or imagination, but, unlike most Pashas of history, quite unbribable. Therefore he is respected and his word goes unquestioned. As he sits there fanning himself and occasionally examining with careful minuteness a watch like a turnip, he can look forth upon the crowds and criminals idling about or awaiting their call, upon the crestfallen and upon the triumphant.

The democratic equality of Islam calls for no outward signs of the law's majesty. And this is true in all walks of life. Even a beggar, craving a boon of the Sultan, though respectful in his mien, will speak to him as to a companion; while a great man, inviting you to dinner, will summon in your servant to feed out of the same dish and will link his fingers in that of the servant to show that hospitality knows no barriers and, incidentally, as a compliment to yourself. It is true that an offender, conscious of his guilt, will prostrate himself three times in the dust before the Pasha, but this is not a sign of inferiority so much as a dumb appeal for mercy; it is play-acting. In the same way, a man ordered to the bastinado will utter loud and heart-rending cries before the first blow falls, though he has privately bribed the mokhazni to strike gently. The democracy of the East is not a self-conscious philosophic conception, it is inherent in the religion of Mohammed. All True Believers are equal before God, not theoretically equal, as in Christianity, but actually equal, and history shows how often the poor man has risen to power and affluence and, conversely, how perilous is the tenure of those born to grandeur. There is envy and scheming in the East, there is treachery, implacability

25

and sudden death, but there is no hushed awe, save in the imminent presence of God, the Merciful, the Compassionate.

I remember going from that court up through the steep alleys of Fez back to my hotel and feeling more than ever as if I were returning from the past into the present, as one returns from the vague strangeness of a dream into approaching consciousness. I do not think I could convey how curious a sensation it was unless I could explain adequately in words the physical atmosphere, the fantastic intricacy, of Fez itself. It is so completely Arabian and so completely mystifying. I never succeeded in grasping its topography. ("Like trying to steer a path through a bowl of macaroni," as a friend once described it.) To the very end I was as lost and fascinated as on the first day. And in all the passion for "improving" places, which is a sign of our own restlessness and moral superiority, let us thank heaven that Fez-el-Bali neither has been, nor can be, modernized. The French, it is true, have introduced electric light, which is an anachronism, but they are not vandals and they know how to leave well alone. To bring Fez up to date would mean, as a preliminary, pulling Fez down. And they have no intention of doing that. The outskirts of the mellah, awful in their sordid vulgarity, house the riff-raff both of Europe and of Africa, while two miles from the city the French have built a pleasant little town for their officials. That

26

is how the problem has been solved. And the result of leaving old Fez alone is that it is now probably the most unspoilt Moslem city in the world.

So let us look at it once more from its protecting sandy cliffs as the sun goes down. Walk out of the city towards the north, past the huge quarry, where the hawks are flying and screaming, past ruined buildings and tombs upon the hillside, and sit here with the city lying beneath you, bathed in light, a fragment of the veritable East. Like one of those enigmatic women who can draw you to her by the promise of something unfathomable and passionate in her still repose, Fez seems to await you at the fall of day. But how often does beauty, in which man, being romantic, is eternally tracing his own ideal of perfection, hide only the cruel egotism of an empty heart? And although the face of Fez be beautiful, her soul is parched. Yet who would not, at this twilight hour, feel the deceptive illusion of complete felicity! Once more the white flags go up, once more the call to prayer resounds over the city, as for twelve hundred years it has resounded in these self-same words, echoed, as it always has been, by the crowing of cocks, as if in brazen challenge of the solemn message. Ah, who would not be at peace, who would not read into the whole scene, as one reads into the eyes of one's beloved, the promise of a great reward.

Adventurous Men

CUNNINGHAME GRAHAM
AMUNDSEN
THE DICTATOR GOMEZ

▽

From a picture of Morocco it seems natural to pass to an account of Cunninghame Graham. For his book, "Mogreb el Acksa," is, so far as I am aware, the most fascinating of all the many books written about that country. And there is still another link: when I went to Morocco, he gave me an introduction to Walter Harris, many years the London "Times" correspondent in Tangier, and I spent there a delightful day with him. As for the other two men of whom I write in this chapter, I need only say that if one adventure leads to another, the thought of one adventurous man leads to thoughts of others.

CHAPTER II

Adventurous Men

Cunninghame Graham

R. B. CUNNINGHAME GRA-
ham was one of the most remarkable men of his period.
At the age of nearly eighty-four he retained not alone
the physical vigour of a man in his prime, but an intellectual curiosity, a youthfulness of outlook, and an eager
interest in affairs that were astonishing. Splendidly
handsome, like an hidalgo of an historic era, it was no
wonder that his friends called him "Don Roberto" and
that he had been more often painted than any other
contemporary figure. The high intelligence and spirit
in his face, combined with the air of breeding and the
good looks, would have made him stand out in any
company and to nobody could the adjective "distinguished" have been more aptly applied.

His bearing was princely. As you entered the room,
he rose with hand outstretched in greeting. Lean and
lithe as a greyhound, he carried his height with the

ease of a man in perfect condition, and in his eye there was already the twinkle of the coming joke. For Don Roberto had his jokes with everybody, jokes bound up, so to speak, with the personality of his hearer, and by reminding you of them at once he helped to create that feeling of comradeship which was one of his charms.

Many a man of fifty would have been exhausted by his varied and ceaseless activities. In spring and early summer he rode every morning in Hyde Park and was to be seen at social functions in the afternoon; in late summer and autumn he moved between England and Scotland, with an occasional visit to Spain; in early winter he led a busy London life; in the New Year he was off to some far corner of the world. Really far: in the last three years he had visited, respectively, South Africa, Ceylon, Brazil and Argentina—where he died.

Famous as an author of rare attainments and a style keen as a rapier, Don Roberto was perhaps even more famous as a man. His life was one long adventure and about his name there lingered the glamour of intrepid achievements. Quite fearless in every sense, he was as much at home in the wildest parts of the earth, riding over the pampas or talking to Moorish chiefs, as in the rough-and-tumble of a political meeting or the barbed politeness of an artistic controversy. But his mingled courage and tact carried him through the diffi- culties of every situation and he was even able to take

Conrad to a Radical meeting and remain friends with him.

Like most genuine writers, Don Roberto was modest about his work, and I never heard him mention it save casually. But he was prodigal in the help he gave other writers and had produced between seventy and eighty Prefaces to oblige his friends. This surely must be a record. If, as he once told me, he had made practically nothing out of his own books, he must have helped other authors to make considerable sums out of theirs. But he did not give it a thought: such deeds were the largesse of his nature, forgotten as soon as granted.

The grand manner, at its finest and simplest, is very disarming, and Don Roberto, head of the clan Graham and rightful Earl of Menteith, had the grand manner to perfection. I should suppose that the thing he valued most in his acquaintances was that sort of imaginative integrity which could see another point of view while holding firm to one's own. His humour was quick, if often rather sardonic, and his stories in the Scottish dialect got down to the very heart of his countrymen. But he had strong powers of moral indignation and I would much rather have been his friend than his enemy. Not that he would have tried to injure one; merely that his tolerance would have melted into such contempt that one would have wilted like a blighted weed.

He was an admirable letter-writer, but as his hand was far from legible, it was not always clear what it was he was saying. Most tantalizing! And in his conversation too—if the analogy be permissible—there was liable to be something one could not quite get at, a kind of aloofness, as if he were drawing one out rather than exchanging confidences. But he was so affable that this was not immediately apparent.

Being singularly free from angularity, he was on easy terms with all sorts of persons, from dukes to Labour M. Ps., from Spanish dons to English stablemen. Both Conrad and Hudson were his close friends —his enquiring spirit had caused him to seek them out in the early days—and the letters they wrote him are amongst the most intimate they ever wrote. I remember we once had an argument as to which of the two had had the more striking personality. He was inclined to vote for Hudson, I for Conrad; but in the end he agreed that they were both so striking that comparisons were useless. His tact, as I have suggested, never failed.

Indeed, I could hardly have imagined him rubbing up anybody the wrong way; and this, I think, was due not only to his inherent courtesy, but to his vivid interest in people of all descriptions. He had even rather a liking for rascals, if they were sufficiently brazen, and we had many a laugh over one such of whom we knew in South America.

34

Though one of the least fanatical of men, Don Roberto had warm sympathies for all oppressed nationalities, just as he had for all who suffered. It was at Conrad's house I first met him—"We must have a bottle of champagne ready for Don Roberto," said Conrad, fearing that he might be fatigued after his long drive from London—and I can never forget how kind he was to me when Conrad died. And at the funeral, grievously distressed though he was himself, he tried to cheer others. I sat next him in the church and as the coffin passed down the aisle he reached across me and touched it: a beautiful and moving gesture of farewell.

All the same, Don Roberto, who had much of the stoic in him, did not wear his heart upon his sleeve. He loved to gather his friends about him—and who, with the exception of ponderous bores, were not his friends?—, he loved the give and take of intelligent talk and was not above those touches of harmless malice which lend spice to conversation. But one was always conscious of an inner silence. What was he really thinking, I sometimes asked myself, and was he having a lot of fun all to himself? I never knew; perhaps nobody ever knew. Despite his friendliness, so open and so generous, he dwelt, it seemed to me, behind an invisible wall.

The last time I saw him was in the summer of 1935, when he called for me at my London flat and drove me to a studio to show me an equestrian statuette of himself which had just been finished. He was immensely pleased with it, especially with the modelling of the horse—throughout his life he had been a great judge of horses—and pointed out its excellencies with all his old ardour. He seemed proud of the feat of having ridden into the studio on horseback, and well he might be.

I thought him looking extraordinarily vigorous, and, indeed, he appeared to grow younger with the years. I fully expected that, like his mother, he would live well into his nineties, for despite a deceptive air of frailty, due to his sparseness and the white halo of his hair, he not only had a magnificent constitution, but found existence, as I have said already, perpetually absorbing and perpetually amusing. Alas, it was not to be! But he had had a long life, and to die in possession of all his faculties, in the enjoyment of an adventurous undertaking, was, beyond question, the death he would have preferred.

Amundsen

About eleven years ago I had the luck to sit at the same table with Captain Roald Amundsen, the Norwegian explorer, on a voyage from Southampton to New York. He was then planning that flight from Spitzbergen to Alaska by airship, which he afterwards made, and he was on his way to the United States to raise money by a lecturing tour.

He had already planted his country's flag at the South Pole and now he was going to see the North Pole. And by doing that, by conquering, as one might say, both the frozen ends of the globe and unveiling the secrets of those icy desolations, he would fulfil his dream and would seek no more adventures in the Arctic or the Antarctic.

At least, that is what he told me. He said that once this journey was accomplished, it was his intention to see something of the tropics and to travel only in the more accessible parts of the world. And I imagine that when he said it, he meant it, for I think that few men knew their minds better than did Amundsen. He had the determination of those unassuming people who map for themselves pathways in the future and do not deviate from them. He was not the kind of man to be a slave to sudden emotional impulses; rather was he the kind whose romantic desires are precise, deeply pondered. To watch his face in repose was to receive an immediate sense of his power to command and of his unyielding resolution. That lined countenance with the great Roman nose, those pale steady eyes, and the almost sombre expression made one think of a brooding bird of prey; but as soon as he smiled all the harshness was gone and its place taken by a look of humour and even gentleness.

37

I feel convinced that when heading an expedition he brooked no opposition and disowned no responsibility, but as a companion in times of leisure no one could have been more friendly or more discreet. He spoke English fluently, though with an accent, and he had certain little exclamations which kept recurring in his talk with the most amusing effect. "Oh, my goodness!" was one of them and "Ja, ja!" was another. He told his stories with animation, but nothing gave him more pleasure, apparently, than to hear other people tell theirs. He was not only a good listener but a good appreciator, and being quite devoid of conceit, he seemed to imagine that the very small feats of the ordinary man were as dynamically arresting as his own almost incredible achievements.

Amundsen was well-informed and interested in many branches of human endeavour. There was nothing of the crank about him, and though he had a natural dignity, nobody enjoyed more a social drink or the aimless chaff of idle hours. Indeed, his sense of humour was almost English in its buoyancy and almost English, too, in the personal touch with which he applied it to the people he liked. And he was very loyal: during his stay in America he went to see his old friend, Dr. Cook, the explorer, who was then doing a prison term for using the mails to defraud. That required moral courage, right enough.

Though past fifty he kept himself conditioned and

38

hard. He walked round and round the boat deck for hours every day and covered over a hundred miles in this manner during the five and a half days' run. It was then, with a congenial companion, that his mind would linger upon reminiscences of former days and then that he would speak of his journey to the South Pole or of the life of the Eskimo or of his home near Oslo, and speak with a familiar touch which seemed to make one almost a sharer of his wanderings.

But with it all he was a reserved man and did not give himself away. One felt, indeed, that he could not have done so to any great extent even had he wished, and that the real passion of his life, the passion for adventure and discovery, had a voiceless quality which was beyond explanation. He was a different, though not more outstanding, type than Selous, the African hunter, who, from the nature of his calling, was almost the only other person I have met with whom I could at all compare him. (I might have added Mr. William Beebe, who explores the depths of the ocean in his bathosphere, Commander Dyott, who has unveiled so many secrets of the Brazilian interior, and Captain Bertram Thomas of Arabian fame, were they not so shadowy in my memory.) For Selous, one sensed, though kindly and modest, was a materialist, whereas Amundsen was, at heart, an idealist. Selous once showed me his huge museum of slaughtered animals; Amundsen once gave me a glimpse of his living dreams. But perhaps, when

39

all is said and done, I do Selous an injustice—if to call a man a materialist is an injustice. He died fighting the Germans in East Africa when he was nearly seventy, and that surely proves an ardent patriotism that had in it an idealistic streak.

But whatever Amundsen's inner self was like, his outer self was full of genial warmth. I recall how when his birthday came round and the captain of the vessel, Arthur—now Sir Arthur—Rostron, himself a man of adventurous spirit and the saviour of the "Titanic" survivors, had arranged for a symbolic menu and a table decorated in his honour, with what delighted pleasure Amundsen kept ordering bottle after bottle of champagne and how the "Oh, my goodnesses!" gushed forth as he surveyed the scene.

These were the interludes which rested his mind. But he was the complete man of action, to whom leisure was merely the surface of existence. If he wrote books and lectured it was only because thus could he fulfil the call which he was for ever hearing. And if neither his books nor his lectures were of any particular account, the explanation is that they were but a means to an end and not the true expression of the man. His true expression was in acts and the true harmony of his life was to be found in the midst of peril and effort.

His death, though heroic and fitting, was surrounded by an atmosphere of tragic irony. He died trying to rescue a man he disliked, Nobile, who was rescued anyhow; he died in the Arctic where he had meant never to go again; he died trusting to aeroplanes, a trust which, as he told me, had saved him once from certain death in these regions. And so I saw him no more and was unable to pay him that visit to Norway which he had asked me to pay him.

The Dictator Gomez

Some eighty miles southwest of Caracas the town of Maracay lies in the wide, fertile valley of Aragua. It is a small town of not more than ten or fifteen thousand inhabitants and yet for years it was the real centre of Venezuela. For there dwelt, for the most part, the Dictator of the country, General Vicente Gomez.

This formidable man, who died so recently, was beyond question the most successfully adventurous figure in the South America of his time. Before he assumed the Presidency in 1910 there had been seventy-two revolutions in about the same number of years: since that date, until his death, there were but three or four abortive attempts. That speaks for itself: at least, in one sense. Ruthless within the limits of dictatorial necessity, domineering, shrewd, possessive, Gomez was yet a great patriot. He gave his country peace, order, financial security. Before his day Venezuela was a byword, now it is highly prosperous.

Of course, the discovery of oil at Maracaibo and the

41

huge royalties paid to the Government on its export enormously strengthened his position. But that was not the ultimate factor of his success. The ultimate factor was his personality, that force of character which could mould men's destinies and command their allegiance. There lay the final secret. A diplomat once said of General Gomez that he impressed him more than did any of the outstanding European statesmen he had met; and no doubt the Dictator, who began life in the humble surroundings of an Andine village, will go down in history as one of those men who, whatever their shortcomings, were gifted with the qualities of the born leader.

Consider some of the results of his rule. The public debt was almost eliminated, Government salaries were regularly paid, and education was encouraged. Modern roads, built on the most approved system and efficiently maintained, pierced into the hinterland, the country was made safe for travellers, and on all sides were apparent the benefits of material progress. Admittedly he grew very rich himself, though most of his wealth was invested locally in houses, coffee haciendas and cattle ranches, but even if he took more than his due share, one cannot but agree that his dictatorship, unlike most of those that went before, was constructive and not destructive.

Certainly it *was* a dictatorship, and dictatorships restrict individual liberty. But then so do democracies. Wherever men congregate together to form govern-

ments liberty is curtailed. If one could not even leave
Venezuela without an official visa, one cannot—if an
alien—even leave the United States without paying
one's Income Tax, while one can scarcely live in England because one has to pay so much.

When I was in Venezuela in 1930 Gomez had retired
from the Presidency—he reassumed it later—and was
then Commander-in-Chief for life, drawing the same
salary as the President and with the Constitution so
altered as to give him very much the same powers.
That was the theory: in reality he was as much of a
Dictator as he had been before. Every week-end the
nominal President, accompanied by members of the
Cabinet, motored from Caracas to Maracay to get his
instructions for the coming week. They might have
been so many office boys for any real initiative they
exercised, and though President Perez was a dignified
figure and relieved the General of many routine duties,
he did not count in the slightest. Nobody counted but
Gomez, nobody at all, and throughout the length and
breadth of Venezuela one name alone was on everybody's lips.

He was feared—some of the more ignorant Negroes
would only refer to him as "The Big Man" lest worse
befall them—, but he was also respected. He stood for
stability in a land whose curse had been instability, and
if he was severe he was generous as well. But he was
devoid of sentiment about movements and his hand

43

fell heavily on those who opposed him. Heavily and sometimes, though not always, cruelly: South American dictators do not wear kid gloves. But give him his due: he did believe in Venezuela. His mental processes might not be invariably easy to follow, but he loved his country. He had never been out of it and he never wanted to go.

His sleepless glance was over everything. It is said that at five each morning telegraphic reports from the Governors of the various Provinces were read to him—read twice by different people in order to avoid all risk of deception—and it is certain that nothing of the least importance happened of which he did not have full cognizance and that no Government move was made which he did not sanction.

His private life was entirely shrouded from foreigners, but on most evenings he would attend the cinema he had had built at Maracay—I have seen him there—and every Sunday morning, between nine and twelve, he used to watch cock-fighting in a barn behind his garage. But his main interests were road-making, forestry, horses and, above all, Venezuela itself.

Maracay was practically an armed camp in my time and the Dictator always had some four thousand troops at his immediate call. But he was simple in his power, and at his rambling house led a kind of patriarchal existence—decidedly patriarchal as to family matters—, whose exact regimen kept him hale in the face of arduous work.

Twice a day he would leave the town to drive to Las Delicias, the estate he had carved out of the wilderness about five miles away. The road was guarded by troops, and a motor wagon, carrying more, followed his car. Altogether, the procession consisted of about a dozen cars, and yet the public, even when the Dictator was there, was allowed to wander about Las Delicias as it pleased. This strange mixture of despotic authority and democratic freedom seemed to suit the Venezuelans. The actuality of the first glided into the semblance of the second, and so long as one kept out of politics one could do pretty well as one chose.

The General was fond of exotic beasts. He had the Zoo removed from Caracas to Las Delicias, where, at the end of the estate, ample enclosures had been constructed for the animals. Fronting the Zoo, by the large space where cars were parked, an open-air café, run by Germans, had been erected, and there the public might drink their beer while watching their ruler. For every evening he held a sort of court alongside the pen of the elephant.

Picture the scene, as I saw it. In the centre chair of a semicircle, under the shade of trees, sits the Dictator in full uniform. On his right is the puppet President of the Republic, and in other chairs are members of the Cabinet, sons and old friends. Military officers and

45

leading citizens hover around; while in front, at a distance of perhaps fifty yards, ordinary people walk to and fro, doffing their hats or bowing low as they pass the Presence.

The General is all animation; he waves his hand to male acquaintances, he rises to greet ladies. Nobody looks less like a dictator. Indeed, with his spectacles and his kindly gestures he has the appearance of a benevolent grandfather. An idyllic dictatorship in an idyllic setting! The dusk is falling, a golden light spreads over field and hill, and at the close of day the aged General rests from his labours, surrounded by his family and his friends.

But make no mistake: he is the master, and he alone. All eyes are fixed on him; at his slightest behest people spring forward; those about him hang upon his every word. In the whole assemblage he is probably the only person completely at his ease—affability itself in the knowledge of undisputed authority. The creator of Las Delicias, relaxed from the cares of state, shares its peaceful beauty with his fellow-citizens, obviously pleased with the scene and gratified by the child of his imagination. As the festooned rows of lamps shine out one after the other, lovely in the gathering gloom, he points towards them as with unaffected delight at the cunning and charming device. At such a moment he is truly like some figure from the antique world, at once the saviour of his country and the father of his people.

46

Suddenly he has risen! At once every one else has risen, too, and every hat is removed—the Dictator is going home. There is a swift bustle of officials, a moving up of the cars, a running forward of the crowd to catch a final glimpse, and in an instant he has been whisked away out of sight. This scene, in such bewildering contrast to what went before, left upon one a singular notion of the General's prestige. It was as if an invisible curtain had been drawn aside to show us his real and feared authority. Almost it made one shiver, as though a sleepy and playful tiger had suddenly bared his claws before bounding into the jungle.

Indeed, no exit of an absolute monarch, in the heyday of mediæval courts, could have been more dramatic than the manner in which the old General used to leave Las Delicias for Maracay when night had come.

Caracas Picture

CITY
SOCIETY

▽

As I have just been writing about Gomez what could be more to the point than to write here about Caracas, the capital of the country over which he ruled so long? Moreover, I am particularly glad to give a glimpse of Venezuela because, having given elsewhere glimpses of Colombia—while Panama was still part of it—and British Guiana, I am filling up, in my own mind at least, a sort of gap. And being on this occasion a guest and so getting the advantage of an inside view, I hope my notes may have some value beyond the mere picturesque.

CHAPTER III

Caracas Picture

City

Deep in the cloudless sky above Caracas the intricate, mazy circling of vultures continues throughout the livelong day. In the hollow of its surrounding hills the city seems to bask in shining peace, its rust-red roofs crowded together, and it is only the interminable, slow sweep of the great birds which suggest that something ominous and insecure which always hangs upon the loveliness of the tropics.

Here and there rise the spires and domes of a Catholic and capital city, breaking the close monotony of one-storeyed houses, and on the outskirts the ramshackle dwellings of the poor meander up the sandy ridges. In the unwinking glare of middle day Caracas, from above, resembles a coloured carving in high relief. The clumps of trees in the suburb of El Paraiso have the stillness of green metal, the palms stand out in moulded symmetry, and the clusters of purple and crimson blossoms look like the splashed paintings of an insane exuberance.

About the whole scene there is, indeed, a touch of magnificent unreality. In some ways the huddled city with its arid slopes reminds one of a Mohammedan town, only here there is no sense of that exhausted age one feels when looking down upon Damascus or upon Fez.

It is natural to search for affinities, for through them we hit upon a formula of expression, but Caracas, with its intense atmosphere of South America, cannot justly be described in terms of other countries or civilizations. There is something exotic and bizarre about it, something impermanent and young, and the dark shadows of its past are, as it were, lost in the dissolving sunlight. The huge mass of the coastal range, blurred by a noontide heat mist, towers abruptly beyond the town, and with its appearance of sombre immortality heightens the dreamlike effect of the city glittering at its foot.

Indeed, it *is* dreamlike, and the very sound of its life, floating upwards in a confused, vast murmur, increases the illusion, as though the city were but a mirage on the sea, a beautiful creation of sun and air and water that would vanish at a breath and die with the imagination which gave it birth.

It is a considerable city of a hundred and thirty-five thousand inhabitants who, with a due proportion of motor-cars and dogs, throng the narrow streets unendingly. Three nationalities predominate, Spanish, Indian and Negro, and in the permutations of their mingled blood a distinct type is emerging.

Of course, there are certain old families, landowners and merchants, of unmixed Latin descent, but they tend to stand more and more aloof, a secluded aristocracy, both from the ruling classes, who are largely a mixture of Spanish and Indian, and from the crowd in general, which, in Caracas at least, runs through the whole gamut of uncertain ancestry.

The people are swarthy, rather small, and sometimes, in youth, extremely good-looking. But the swift maturity of the tropics carries a sting in its tail, and in a few years these pretty girls, sitting by open windows level with the road to watch the passers-by, will have grown fat and unattractive. Time's revenge!

The houses are washed in pale pinks, greens or yellows. Cool patios, simpler than those of Seville, but constructed on a similar model, open through arched passageways, and ancient churches, with elaborate façades, are a reminder of the Spanish dominion. In the olden times Caracas was never one of the great centres of government, like the cloud-cities of Bogota or Quito, and its memorials are consequently fewer; but the touch of other centuries still rests upon it, and many of its obscurer houses were built in the heyday of Spanish rule.

But to the Venezuelan its chief glory is as the home

53

of South American liberty. Such men as Miranda, Bolivar—his house in Caracas is a national museum— Sucre and Paez were born in Venezuela, and Caracas was the lodestar of the earliest revolts. No wonder the inhabitants have delighted to honour their heroes. Every square of the city has its statue, and even in the splendid avenues of the southern outskirts, where the trees meet overhead as in a leafy glade and the glowing colours of bougainvillæa, flamboyant and hibiscus interlace the green, each crossroad has its statue dedicated to the theme of freedom. The Liberators, too, saw the hummingbirds flutter about the purple orchids, and it is fitting that their bronze figures should now reign for ever over that unchanging scene.

I might add here that there is also a statue of Henry Clay, the protagonist of South American liberty, in Caracas. Some years ago the United States Congress voted forty thousand dollars for this purpose, and it is, I believe, the only occasion on which Congress has provided funds to erect a statue of an American in a foreign land.

Government offices and public institutions fill whole blocks of the city. Their architecture is, in the main, too ornate to be pleasing, but the courts of the University have an air of peace and the great courtyard of the Capitolia, with its central fountain, possesses a real dignity. Caracas is made gay by numerous, well-kept municipal gardens, and if from above it bears a Moorish aspect, a nearer view from the hilly section of El Calvario suggests rather an Italian town of the Middle Ages, with its weathered roofs, its scattered trees, its steep narrow streets, its cobbled pavements.

But here, again, one must not be misled. No European city, no city out of the tropics, ever had a market like that of Caracas. How can one describe this tumultuous spectacle, which holds, in concentrated essence, the very colour and scent of the South? Mules from the country stand in patient rows, exquisite birds in tiny cages are being sold on the curb, and in front of the buildings are heaped masses upon masses of flowers. And not only the blooms of the tropics, but scarlet gladioli, white lilies and daisies, roses of every hue. Upon the mountain side are market gardens, and there Italians cultivate the flowers and vegetables of the North.

All this is as nothing to what awaits one within. A seething crowd, piles of outlandish fruits, smells enticing in one spot, repulsive in the next, huge, dull-eyed fish, tethered turkeys, slabs of meat, local pottery—everything one might least and most expect. And it has an "atmosphere," that thing which words cannot catch save by the chance inspiration of created imagery.

One can buy most goods in Caracas, for the shops are crammed with the merchandise of Europe and the United States, but living is expensive and money melts with its usual painful rapidity. However, the visitor

55

should not go to Caracas to acquire things, but rather to acquire experience. The South America of one's imaginings here comes to life. Grave señors, dressed all in black, salute one another with shoulder pattings; soldiers, with rifles between their knees, sit beside the barracks; khaki-clad policemen regulate the traffic with flourishes of their batons.

All is suave and orderly as in a modern city going about its daily business—but to what extent is this civilisation a veneer? South America is a strange place, and the incalculable, cruel heart of the wilderness is never far away. How can one really know this town or these people? How can one tell what is happening beneath the surface? (These questions were asked on the strength of my 1930 visit: the riots and the plunderings of 1936 supply an answer.)

In a direct line Caracas is only six or seven miles from the sea, but its altitude is three thousand feet and it takes the train an hour and a half to wind up round the mountains from La Guaira. The Conquistadores chose well; though, indeed, their aim was security from attack rather than protection from the heat. Save in the very middle of the day, the temperature is never oppressive. The early mornings are pleasant and a coolness falls in the late afternoon.

That is the ideal hour. Fleeting shadows play upon the deeper violet of the mountains and a deceptive glow gilds all the failing dusk. Frogs wake in the pools, fresh odours fill the air. And presently the encircling lights begin to shine out one by one and the deep softness of tropical dark enfolds the world.

In the city itself the sellers of lottery tickets have ceased their cries and friends are greeting one another in the lit-up wine shops which stand open at every corner. The crowds have increased rather than lessened, for Southern blood craves company, but there is a universal sense of ease after the toil of day.

And for the traveller approaching from afar, night, with its erasing hand, leaves nothing but the tiered lamps to show a city of enchantment. A sea fog, gliding high upon the hill, has dimmed the immediate stars, but Caracas, combed free of matter, gleams in the darkness like a fabulous jewel upon a jet-black coronet.

Society

Venezuelan and foreign society in Caracas revolve in separate spheres, and though they touch upon one another with friendly impact, their orbits are essentially independent. Of course, there are foreign families who, through long residence or intermarriage, have an assured footing in both camps, but generally speaking the attitude towards social usage is subtly different in the two, and the meetings between them, however cordial, have an air of formality.

One must know a Venezuelan family very well before

being asked to anything more than an afternoon tea, and though Venezuelans are frequently encountered at the dinners given by Europeans and Americans, they have a tendency, even there, to group themselves together and enjoy their own gossip and their own jokes. This is not through gaucherie, for their manners are perfect, their knowledge of the world considerable, and their clothes of the smartest, but rather through a kind of clannishness, a kind of inherent inability to mingle easily with strangers.

The "best families" of Caracas are, for the most part, closely connected, and Venezuelan society is a sort of intimate circle. The very nature of its construction prevents the foreigner from penetrating to its core; and though he will be received with politeness, he cannot be given the password.

And it must be understood that, however rich a Venezuelan may be, he will probably employ but a few slovenly Venezuelan servants, with the result that much of the housework has to be done by the family and that entertaining on a grand scale is practically impossible. If, however, one is fortunate enough to be asked to a Venezuelan luncheon party, one is assured of lavish hospitality.

Let me describe such a meal given by the grandsons of the famous President-Dictator of other days, Guzman Blanco, at their country hacienda. It lies about forty-five miles from Caracas, in a valley of sugar-cane and palm, and their house is a rambling old building in the Colonial style.

On this bright Sunday morning not fewer than twenty cars are drawn up outside it. In one corner of the balcony hired cantadores are playing and singing the high-pitched national airs, and a few couples are performing the juropa, a dance at once graceful and energetic. At the other side a crowd of Venezuelans and foreigners is talking voluble Spanish, while individuals wander about the lower rooms or find their way to the cocktail table in the back courtyard.

A feeling of go-as-you-please, slightly embarrassing to one who is not even on the outer rim, pervades all, but that is the Venezuelan courtesy of wanting you to feel at home. In appearance the party is an informal one, but actually it is a very unusual honour. Such parties are, indeed, the high-water mark of Venezuelan esteem.

Underneath the trees are trestles laden with food. An ox, killed and roasted that day, is brought on; the meat, cut into shapeless hunks, is strung on long skewers and one is supposed to slice off pieces for himself. As a prelude to a meal it is not artistic, while the resulting sights are positively barbaric. To watch gentlemen gnawing at large bones held between their hands is rather suggestive of a cannibal feast, and it did not encourage my appetite.

But there is plenty of food of a more delicate nature;

59

for example, ayjacas, which resemble bloated pancakes and are filled with minced meat, raisins and olives: the Mexican tamale is their first cousin and they are excellent. No bread is provided; its place is taken by rolled lumps of cold, pounded maize, each one served, like a cob, in a wrapper of maize leaves. It is a highly unpalatable substitute and could only be swallowed, so far as one of the guests was concerned, by covering it thick with the fiery Venezuelan pickle, of which great dishes are scattered about the table. The cakes that terminate this open-air banquet may be called its only European touch, if one excepts the Scotch whiskey and soda, a drink as popular in South America as elsewhere.

To understand Venezuelan society one would have to understand the psychology of Venezuelans. And that is not a simple matter. Their affinities with us are misleading, for their views on life, while less complex in some respects, have the obscurity of a national outlook inherited from several civilizations and modulated by the special circumstances of their history.

The Venezuelans, and more particularly the women, are delightful people, full of swift intelligence and social nuance, but it may be doubted whether many of them have intellectual interests. In the unrestful drama of their life love and recreation are the principal anodynes.

They accept existence fatalistically, and without being exactly vivacious have yet learnt to take things as they come and not probe too deeply beneath the crust. The need for discretion in a country which has known innumerable revolutions, with all those sudden changes of fortune which are the corollary of upheaval, has found its recompense in a rather caustic wit. Punctilious in their behaviour, Venezuelans are, nevertheless, quick at repartee and at the invention of telling nicknames.

Venezuela, like all Latin countries, abounds in conventional social observances. There is only one of these which calls for comment here and that is the custom of sending magnificent bouquets or baskets of flowers to mark any complimentary event. On returning from abroad or on giving an entertainment a lady will receive these gorgeous tokens of goodwill, and for days on end her home will bloom like a hothouse.

But though the habits of the country naturally tinge the lives of Americans and Europeans living in Venezuela, yet it is surprising to what an extent, as I have pointed out, they dwell in a world of their own. It is an extraordinarily hospitable world, peopled by exiles who instinctively hold together, and if one knows the "right set"—a term possibly of elastic interpretation in the variety of sets, but more probably of absolute value —a holiday in Caracas is one of the most agreeable of experiences.

Putting aside the usual round of gaiety and sport— dining and dancing, golf and tennis, swimming at one

country club and clay-pigeon shooting at another—
there is, above all, a peculiar friendliness in the atmosphere, though this is perhaps rather superficial. It is
as though people thrown too much together had resolved to overcome the inevitable tension by making
more allowances for others and by yielding less to their
own idiosyncrasies. If it be a counsel of perfection to
advise most people to arise hungry from a meal, it is
a truism to tell them that when they leave Caracas they
will be hungry for more.

In the suburb of El Paraiso there are many stately
white houses, surrounded by tropical gardens. Some
of these houses are Foreign Legations, others are the
homes of wealthy merchants or of political agents of the
oil companies. Where the residents are non-Venezue-
lans the domestic servants are almost entirely West
Indians, natives of Trinidad, St. Lucia or Martinique,
and the routine is managed with remarkable efficiency.
Some of these cooks, indeed, can turn out a dinner that
could hardly be bettered, and in such a house the service
will be attuned to do it justice.

El Paraiso, in its wooded beauty, is not inaptly
named, and on one of those nights when a dance is being
given and the perfumed garden is alive with lamps, the
observing stranger might well wonder whether this be
not, indeed, a veritable earthly paradise. Music sounds
beyond the wall, strolling couples pass in and out of

the shadows, and white-robed footmen, dim and silent as great moths, glide here and there.

Beneath the surface, maybe, all is not unruffled, for mankind is born to trouble, but looked at as a picture, the scene is as exquisite as a painting by Watteau.

Figures
of Yesterday

MEREDITH
WATTS-DUNTON
WILLIAM ROSSETTI

▽

*In complete contrast there may lie
a sort of inverted link, and that is
why I am bold enough to put this
chapter here. I never heard the
three men of whom I now write so
much as mention South America—
not even Meredith had his Brazilian, as did Balzac—but (to go back
one chapter further) authors also
are adventurers. All rather far-
fetched, but better than nothing.
Meredith, Watts-Dunton and William Rossetti have been dead for
years. In the normal course, the
number of people who knew them
must be lessening rapidly and it is
pleasant to look back and recall
their personalities.*

CHAPTER IV

Figures of Yesterday

Meredith

IN MY YOUTH I REGARDED George Meredith not alone as the greatest of living writers, but as one of the greatest of all writers. I used to carry about with me the two little red cloth volumes of his collected poems and bore people intolerably by insisting that they see in them what I saw in them. It is difficult to revive even the memory of such an ardour, especially as I feel sure that I could not now read many of his poems, despite magical lines in "Love in the Valley," or any of his novels; but so intense was it that I actually wrote, as my first book, a study of his works. Fortunately nothing is quite so dead as a dead book, and that labour of love has now vanished from the consciousness of mankind. If this be doubted, I need only remark that Mr. Hugh Walpole, whose knowledge of books is as vast as his library, once lost a bet, I have been informed, by asserting that no such book had ever been written.

Meredith, who was then nearly eighty, was not at all enthusiastic at the idea of another volume about him—as he wrote to me before it was published, "My fear in this case is that as regards rewards for the work, you will have expended time and labour fruitlessly"—, but at any rate, he was not hostile. Indeed, he might have been called benevolently neutral and he even asked me down to Boxhill to have tea with him, although I must admit that I fished for the invitation.

I recall that visit well and yet as through a kind of haze. When I made it, my spiritual temperature was above normal, and that tends both to intensify and to blur at one and the same moment. It was a wintry afternoon, but to me the bleakness of the weather meant nothing at all. My heart was pounding as I strode up from the station at Burford Bridge and knew that at last I was going to *enter* that cottage, on which I had so often enviously gazed, and going to *see* George Meredith, whose name epitomized for me all that was glamourous in life. And then, incredibly, I was through the gate and walking up the short drive, and there, above the garden slope, was the châlet in which he had done so much of his writing. No, such emotions are not to be recovered!

Outwardly it was an uneventful meeting, but I was not living in the external world. Face to face with Meredith, I seemed to float upon the air of romance and to taste the very savour of genius. How I clung to

68

the minutes, how I longed to say something that would really make him understand what his books had meant to me!

It was a small room in which he received me, a room furnished in the unostentatious style of a suburban villa, and the table was littered with French newspapers. Meredith sat in an armchair beside the fire and after a time his son arrived and sat opposite him in the other armchair. They were both as agreeable to me as they could be, though I imagine that these visits from obscure enthusiasts must have been an infernal nuisance.

Why the actual conversation has mostly gone beyond recall I cannot say, unless it be that I was drinking in the atmosphere too greedily to bother with mundane things; but I do remember his speaking with pleasure of an American engineer who had recently been to call on him on his way to Siberia and to whose return visit he was looking forward. And, of course, there were enquiries about myself, social talk—the usual trifles by which a great man strives to make easy the worshipping speechlessness of a disciple.

In profile, with his white hair and beard set off by a scarlet tie, with his exquisitely chiselled features, Meredith was extremely handsome—his distinguished voice fitted absolutely with his appearance—, but full-face he was by no means so impressive. He was conscious of this, I believe, and much preferred to sit in an advantageous position. But if he was vain, he assuredly had something to be vain about: into old age he carried with him—sideways—the look of a Greek god.

All too soon the visit ended and I was out on the drive once more. I was elated at what had happened, I was depressed that it was over, and the rest of the day is a blank. And I never saw him again. I presume that, unlike the American, I left no faintest impression behind. It saddened me at the time, for I had much hoped that I would do so, but perhaps it was just as well. Within the next year or two my enthusiasm began gradually to wane and when I attended his funeral in 1909—I can see his daughter now, a stoutish figure in deep black, carrying the urn which contained his ashes up the aisle of the little local church—I had to whip up a sentiment I no longer truly felt. Perhaps a youth should never beard his hero.

And yet, I imagine, I underrate his capacity now as much as I overrated it once. He was a writer of unusual, if often distorted, power, and though I can hardly agree with the remark Henry James once made to a friend of mine, "Meredith does the best things best," still he certainly could rise to rare heights of eloquence and poetry.

Watts-Dunton

Theodore Watts-Dunton was a figure of literary importance in his day. True, his fame was largely a reflected glory from that of Swinburne, with whom he shared a house for the better part of thirty years, but in his own right he was also a figure. He delivered critical judgments of a magisterial sweep; he coined the phrase "The Renaissance of Wonder"; he was the author of a novel of gypsy life which enjoyed an enormous vogue at one time; and he was even a poet.

But Swinburne has been dead these many years; the reviews Watts-Dunton wrote are mostly buried in the files of the old "Athenæum"; phrases have their hour; perhaps not one single person is now agitated by *Aylwin*; and as for his poems, well, I can only say that, on receiving from him a copy of the collected edition and on noting that the effusion I was about to read opened thus, "I cannot brook thy gaze, beloved bird," I softly closed the volume. Why spoil the effect of so perfect a line by looking farther?

In brief, Watts-Dunton is now practically forgotten. And yet he was, in a sense, the dean of English letters and young men used to journey down to the Pines, Putney Hill, partly with the idea of hearing his views, but more particularly, it must be admitted, in the hope of meeting Swinburne.

I was one of those young men, but though Watts-Dunton was always promising to introduce me to the author of *Poems and Ballads*—he was going to arrange a dinner—he never did. But then he never did anything. It was not that he made consciously false promises, but simply that he was England's champion procrastinator. His inability to get things done amounted almost to an obsession. It reminded one of those nightmares in which the busier and more energetic one is, the more hopelessly muddled and involved one becomes. It was very odd: he was not lazy; indeed, there was a sort of buzzing industriousness about him—, but nothing ever happened. That, of course, is a slight exaggeration, but it was the effect he produced. After all, he did finish *Aylwin* at last, but I am assured that for years and years before it was published paragraphs used to appear in the press saying that it was almost ready. No book, I gather, ever received so much free publicity over so long a period.

Even in the tiniest matters he procrastinated to an extent that was inconceivable. Somebody once gave me a rare Swinburne pamphlet, and Watts-Dunton, who was the most obliging of men, told me that he would get the bard to autograph it for me. But he kept putting it off and off, then to his dismay he mislaid the pamphlet, and after his death it was found lying about at the Pines, unsigned.

Physically, Watts-Dunton was very small, with a large head and a drooping grey moustache. He had a curious crawling walk and when he entered the room he produced somehow, hugging the wall as he did, the illusion of a crab warily approaching its victim. But no comparison could have been more false in actuality, for he was a charmingly friendly old man and never exhibited a trace of condescension. He tried to make one feel at home immediately, and yet there was something strange about him, as if he lived inside a huge, unreal bubble. One felt that to him a listener was an audience rather than a personality and that the instant one left one would be utterly forgotten in the reverberation of his own soliloquies.

Once, I remember, he mistook me for Mr. W. B. Yeats—not much of a compliment as regards age, however complimentary in another direction—and announced mellifluously that he had read "all my beautiful plays." I explained as gently as I could that I was not Mr. Yeats and had written no plays. Watts-Dunton accepted the explanation with his usual urbanity, but later on again observed that he had read all my plays. I feebly protested once more, but though he was as gracious as ever I doubt whether it registered.

I mention this episode as proof of the impersonality of his mind: he wanted me to be Yeats and therefore I *was* Yeats. And yet he could be very astute on occasion and I have sometimes wondered whether his apparent vagueness did not conceal a settled policy.

Now and then, when sitting with him, I would try to swing the conversation round to Swinburne—it was thrilling to visualize how on the very next floor the poet was probably composing at that moment—, but Watts-Dunton did not respond with marked enthusiasm. Of course, one of the objects of his life was to keep intruders from Swinburne, who was stone deaf and immoderately excitable, but I formed the notion that, apart from any protective feeling, he regarded it as rather tactless to talk much about Swinburne when there was Watts-Dunton to talk to.

And incidentally, he was a good talker, a very good talker, if one could but adjust oneself to that other-world mood in which he seemed to dwell and appreciate that to him a monologue constituted the art of conversation. He had a real love of literature, to which he had graduated from an intensely dilatory career as a lawyer of authors, and I recall how on one occasion he recited to me a long passage from, I assume, Shakespeare, as three different persons, in three different epochs, would have recited it. His diction was dramatic, indeed, melodramatic, but on the whole I felt more uncomfortable than elated. I am not at all sure that I ever quite understood the point he was trying to make. At any rate, I have totally forgotten it now.

Finally, tea would be announced and Watts-Dunton would come down to earth again. He was evidently fond of tea and I never saw any one eat so much hot buttered toast at a sitting. He must have had an iron digestion. In a way, so hearty an appetite was incongruous in that room, with its Pre-Raphaelite pictures, its books overflowing on to tables and the floor itself, its whole air of scholarly pursuits and dusty untidiness; but on second thoughts I feel that it gave a homely touch of reality to what, both as to its aspect and its owner, seemed to suggest a neglected, queer old museum.

Peace to his ashes! He was a unique personality if not a great writer, and I can never forget his forbearing kindness to a callow youth whose visits, so patiently borne, may very well have appeared to him entirely uncalled-for.

William Rossetti

I knew William Rossetti, the brother of Dante Gabriel and Christina Rossetti, for nearly twenty years. He was seventy-two when I first met him—it was through my brazen cheek in writing to ask him for some autographs of his family and circle and his characteristic kindness in sending me a whole bundle—and eighty-nine when he died, and during all that long period he invariably treated me with the utmost consideration and courtesy.

Indeed, one of the things which set him apart was his unruffled courtesy. It descended on all alike; it exalted one's self-esteem and awoke a resolve to be at one's best. Such courtesy is very unusual and it is a singular fact— singular from the diversity of persons and places—that I think I have only seen it in this fine flower in Joseph Conrad, in an Anglican Bishop I met in London, in a South African Judge I met in Pretoria and in a British Vice-Consul I met in Cerro de Pasco, in the Peruvian

Andes. And even so, I must make reservations: Conrad had his attacks of gouty irritability and I knew the other three men but slightly. But William Rossetti I knew very well, and he was as courteous at the finish as at the beginning.

I used to stay with him and his family for weeks on end, and the hours I spent dozing or reading on the huge sofa on which Shelley passed his last night on earth constitute a shameless record of downright laziness. But though they were wasted hours in one sense, they were precious hours in another. They helped me more and more to appreciate that astounding man who, while extremely prosaic in some directions, had yet about him an air of true distinction. The simplicity of his character embraced a fine nobility of spirit, and without being himself original, he was sympathetic to originality. The wide range of his artistic interests showed the culture of his mind and throughout his life he had kept the trust and friendship of turbulent geniuses. That is a tribute both to his loyalty and to the quality of his imaginative insight.

His days went by like clockwork and he was as methodical as a machine. One could tell to a minute when he would be down every morning, when he would enter his study—the most fascinating little book-lined room, whose window opened on to a neglected garden where cats were always prowling and scratching—, when he would have his first pipe, when he would settle to work and when he would stop, when he would go in his slouch hat and poet's cloak, a real figure out of the past, for his afternoon walk across Primrose Hill, and when he would retire for the night.

All was arranged to suit the instinctive orderliness of his being, and even his appearance, with his grey beard, dark old-fashioned clothes, and quiet eyes, suggested that calm which comes from an existence in harmony with its surroundings. His papers and letters were neatly docketed according to the years, he bound up pamphlets and catalogues in innumerable volumes with a view to preserving such ephemera for the interest of future generations, and when he bought a new edition of the *Encyclopædia Britannica* at about eighty he began to read it right through from A to Z, omitting only the mathematical articles.

He was, indeed, an omnivorous reader both of Italian and of English—Dante, Shelley and Walt Whitman were constantly on his lips—, but though I tried to get him to appreciate Conrad, it was of no avail. Modern in a sense, through his lack of the usual prejudices, nevertheless his interest in literature stopped at Swinburne, who was one of his oldest friends. He seldom visited the poet of recent years, but on hearing that he was ill, he hurried down to Putney, only to find that he had died half an hour before. He saw him lying on his bed, noble and grand, and I think that nothing for a generation had stirred him so deeply.

77

Latterly Rossetti never left London, but all sorts of people would come to pay their respects. The most famous man I ever encountered at his house was Holman Hunt, white-bearded, frail, practically blind. It was touching to watch Rossetti lead him by the hand and to hear him murmur, "My dear old friend." Some of the people who used to call struck me as being eccentric to the point of madness, but Rossetti endured them, every one, with his patient courtesy. He disliked abstract or futile discussions, and being, at once, perfect in his politeness and tenacious in his views, would frequently listen with an appearance of interest which he did not feel. But he never hurt anyone's susceptibilities and the worst he would say of a departed guest would be, "I regard him as fanciful" or "He teazes me"—which last, in the Rossettian phraseology, meant very definitely and strongly, "He wearies me by his talkativeness and extravagance."

Although grave and gentle in his deportment, William Rossetti had a sense of humour. At a joke which he appreciated a charming smile would mantle his face and it was delightful to watch him with his granddaughter, Imogen. The graciousness of his manner was a reflection of his personality, and of only one person did I ever hear him speak with real bitterness. That one person was Oscar Wilde, and while this dislike may have been due to an inborn antipathy, I suspect that at some time or other Wilde must have made a flippant remark about him or about the Rossettis as a family.

But speaking generally, he was the most placid of men and could get on with anybody. He even remarked of a tiresome old tippler who used to haunt the place, saying nothing of the least interest but perpetually puffing out his cheeks, "I have a regard for ———." He had known many sorrows and many troubles, but until the last few years, when physical disabilities increased upon him, he was entirely serene and I recollect his telling me, at the age of eighty-two, that he would be quite content to live on Tristan da Cunha, provided he had sufficient books.

Whether he would really have been content may be doubted, for if ever a house and its owner had grown together, so to speak, it was William Rossetti and 3 St. Edmund's Terrace. The impress of his personality lay upon the muffled rooms, and as soon as one set foot over the threshold, one felt transported not merely in atmosphere but in time itself. An indescribable sensation, as if one had escaped into some other world. The old house was as reposeful as its old owner, and with its portraits by D. G. Rossetti, its Japanese prints, its china and its cabinets seemed to drowse away the days in silence.

Although Rossetti was cheerful in himself, he was philosophically a pessimist, and his mild face had a melancholy caste. He was invariably gloomy as to national events and when the War broke out felt sure that the Germans would win. An amusing instance of this instinctive pessimism occurred one day when he and his daughter, Helen, and I, who were staying in the Channel Islands, went for a day's excursion from Guernsey to Sark. In due course the hour for return arrived, but while Rossetti and his daughter safely boarded the steamer, I, who was a little behind, reached the shore only to find that the gangway had been raised. Rossetti, standing by the rail, was but a few feet from me, and I made energetic signs to him to draw someone's attention to my plight; but for all answer he continued to gaze at me with despairing commiseration, audibly announcing in tones of deepest gloom, "Poor, unfortunate fellow!" He felt convinced that all efforts would be useless and that I was inevitably stranded for the night, if not, indeed, for ever. However, I did manage to get on board, but even now when I think of his woebegone expression and picture how he just stood there without doing anything, I cannot help laughing.

He had the most amazing memory, and not only for great events but for things long since forgotten by everybody else. And he was so imperturbably good-natured, not to say benign, that one felt an almost irresistible desire to draw him out. One would ask him, for example, whether he remembered anything about some obscure murder which happened in 1858. In answer he would first say, "Let me reflect," and then presently he would begin like this: "On the tenth day of October, 1858, a servant girl, named Harriet Welbore, employed by a family at Twickenham, opened the front door at seventy thirty-five in order to take in, as usual, the morning supply of milk, when she perceived, lying in a pool of blood," and so on, and so on. I am not exaggerating in the least; that is precisely how he did talk. It was astonishing, and sounded all the more astonishing because of the resonant modulations of his voice.

But he was totally unaware of any special gift in this, as in any other, direction. Indeed, he was as completely without—vanity is too strong a word, self-esteem would perhaps be better—as he was without jealousy. I recall how once, when I had been reading a long narrative poem of his written many years before and had made the comment that two lines in it appeared to me to be superior to the rest, he answered with the utmost equanimity, "These were the only lines in the poem written by Gabriel."

It was all part of his simplicity, and in this respect I remember how he said to me on one occasion, "I have always had the utmost dislike for physical pain," as if it were not necessarily a universal experience but an original idea. But every remark he uttered came from him with so stately a grace and entire lack of affectation that, whether it made you think or smile, it somehow made you love him the more.

81

And perhaps it was his simplicity which caused him to be so amusingly literal now and again. On being given a copy of Mr. Norman Douglas's *Fountains in the Sand,* with the information that it had to do with Tunisia, he immediately, in perverse matter-of-factness, assumed what its contents were, and observed that he considered the title irrational. "Why didn't he call it *Irrigation in Tunisia?*" he asked with faint petulance.

As I mentioned above, he lost his serenity, though never the sweetness of his nature, during the closing years of his life. He felt heavily the burden of his great age and he used to say to me, "I should regard it as a disaster if I were to live to be ninety." Well, he missed the disaster by a few months, dying peacefully from exhaustion following on a chill, but he did live long enough to see England victorious. And that, I am told, cheered him at the end.

I have known more exciting people than William Rossetti, but I have never known one kinder or more straightforward, one more free from the meaner weaknesses of humanity. As a writer he was pedestrian, but as a man he soared.

Two English Scenes

GHOSTS IN CORNWALL
ECLIPSE IN YORKSHIRE

▽

*English authors bring back one's
mind to English scenes, and I hope,
therefore, that this chapter, coming
where it does, may be held to jus-
tify itself. Cornwall and Yorkshire
are nearly as far apart as two English
counties can be, but both have their
particular charms for those who
know them, and if, in the Yorkshire
section, there is little description of
the countryside, the Cornish section
is little else but description. I have
written briefly in another book of
Kent and Northumberland, very
favourite counties of mine, and at
greater length about London; and
now, I suppose, I have said enough.*

CHAPTER V

Two English Scenes

Ghosts in Cornwall

THE VILLAGE OF LELANT lies at the narrowest point of Cornwall, with the English Channel a few miles to the south and an estuary of the Atlantic at its very door. It is a typical Cornish hamlet, windy and steep, and its inhabitants, with their dark Celtic faces, show at a glance that you are no longer in Saxon England. The receding water leaves the estuary one broad expanse of mud, glistening with shallow pools, and at night the cries of wading birds can be heard afar, thrilling and wild, in the stillness of the sleeping village.

There is little to ruffle the surface of life in that secluded place. The echo of towns sounds no louder than the ripple of the tide brimming into the estuary and all their unrest seems blown away by the fresh sea-wind coming to one sweetly over the upland pastures.

I would not call the contours of the country particularly striking, but they are, at least, free from the artificiality of recognized beauty spots—not artificial in themselves, by and large, but artificial through our preconceived attitude towards them—and at times they have about them a curious touch of strangeness, as if there was something haunted in the very spirit of the land. It comes to one very faintly, that touch, like an echo of things which happened long, long ago, like a memory attenuated almost to nothingness down countless centuries, like the impalpable, vague feeling of sorrow which lingers around the walls of ancient houses.

I do not know how to describe it, so faint and strange it is, but I did just feel it, a voiceless whisper, amid the sunken barrows of a prehistoric race that crown the rocky summit of Tren Crom. A fair, wide landscape opened on every side, a Cornish landscape of cultivated fields with farms along the rise, but on the brow of the hill the imagination was haunted by a sense of eeriness. Shaded valleys and starless nights suggest to the untutored mind the proper setting for ghostly visitations, but it is at noonday on hill-tops that fear can really steal upon one. It was there, in the night of time, that our ancestors had their dwellings, there that they sleep now for ever. And it is there, if anywhere, that their shades keep watch and the imprint of their wizardry hangs upon the breeze. Savages know the feeling: to them mountains are of dread import, the home of spirits which must not be disturbed.

But suppose that, after all, there are no ghosts in Cornwall and that the whole sensation is simply an illusion created by the wish. Does that differ so much from most of our realities, which are only another form of illusion? In the whirlpool of to-day's eddying values who can put his finger upon absolute truth?

Tren Crom is situated but a few miles from Lelant and driving thither one passes through narrow lanes lying between tangled hedges. The Cornish hedge is a stone wall covered with earth and seeded thick with flowers and shrubs. There are no such hedges elsewhere, hedges which hold the very essence of summer in their rich profusion.

These lanes will open ever and anon upon waste spaces riddled with abandoned tin workings, and to come on them gave me an odd, exotic feeling, as if I were motoring again through the Malay States. And, indeed, there *is* something exotic about Cornwall. In many respects it resembles an ordinary English county, but then suddenly one sees how entirely different it is from the remainder of England. Its inhabitants feel no more English than they look—the English are "foreigners" to them and a tradesman will say in all seriousness, "I must send to England for that"—, its hills are steeped in timeless mysteries, palms grow in sheltered coves, people salute one another by raising the arm, and visitors come to admit at last that there *is* a kind of hidden queerness about the land.

87

I attempt no explanation, but presumably the country is saturated in Celtic tradition. When, at Marazion, I looked out upon St. Michael's Mount, washed by its green waves, it was as if I were looking upon some magic Celtic isle famous in chivalry and song. Viewed from farther along the coast, in the mist of a dull afternoon, it seems to melt into the Channel like some legendary castle rock which had arisen there through the mere force of subconscious memory. It cannot compare in picturesqueness with its French counterpart, Mont St. Michel in Brittany, but it is more elfin. It is as if it held a story older than any records and, like the mainland of Cornwall itself, was fanned by the breath of a vanished civilization.

As night begins to fall, the shrouded Channel, lying fold on fold in the direction of the Lizard, assumes an aspect of deep repose, as though everlasting rest had settled upon that dangerous coast. A fleet of fishing boats, their sails very dark against the afterglow, is making for Penzance, whose lamps glimmer and twinkle low down along the shore. All is still: the dim land and the dim water, sunk in dreams of old kingdoms and of cruel storms, are hushed at the decline of day; and the quiet air, full of sea murmurs and sweet scents, is touched with beatitude after the age-long ravage of time and tide. Such is a summer night in Cornwall.

And perhaps that is how we ought to leave it. In-

88

deed, I would feel inclined to stop at this moment did I not remember so vividly an afternoon when I sat above the cliffs of Land's End and gazed upon that watery highway which leads, beyond the hazy rim, to the enticing places of the world. Land's End! Yes, it is there, most of all, there at the very toe of England, that one ought to say good-bye to Cornwall.

On that day of perfect calm, between the boundless expanse of pale blue heavens and deep blue ocean, it seemed almost to me, immersed as I was in a reverie of travel, as if out of the dazzling veil of the sun's track there might suddenly emerge, distinct and far, a coral island with palms along its beach, ringed with white foam beyond a rainbow sea. And that, again, shows how Cornish spells had ensnared me.

A little steamer was passing northwards outside the line of rocks on which the Longships lighthouse stands, while inshore, witness to last night's storm, great flakes of spume, lace-like in their traceries, undulated on the dying swell. The sound of the breaking sea, regular and vibrant, was borne up from below, and the shadow of sailing gulls crossed and recrossed the rough, short heath of the summit. And away to the south-west, vigilant in its lonely gauntness, towered the stack of the Wolf, guarding sleeplessly the entrance to the English Channel. It was a scene of fullness and of peace. Thought, quickened by the entrancing loveliness of the day, stirred upon the outward splendour, as though to find there the secret of that harmony which shall explain all and make all things live.

I suppose that, despite "good-byes," I shall keep going back to Cornwall—I have actually been there since writing this and have looked down on Tintagel on just such an afternoon; but I do not suppose that I shall ever recover the emotions of that first (well, not first exactly, but first receptive) visit. And that is only to be expected. In a world of living men what room is there for hints so intangible and enigmatic that one is always expecting something which never happens, just as in a twilit hall one occasionally seems to hear a half-whisper which for ever eludes one. Let the old Cornish dead keep to themselves: we shall all be joining them before so very long.

Eclipse in Yorkshire

I have on various occasions started out on long and exciting journeys, journeys that were to take me to the uttermost parts of the earth, but I have seldom had more the feeling of adventure than when setting forth from King's Cross Station on the evening of June 28th, 1927, for the run up to Yorkshire. For at that moment I was, if I may so put it, starting out on a journey into the depths of the sky, into the vast spaces of the heavens, with the hope of witnessing something which had not been witnessed in England for more than two hundred years. Romance depends upon the angle of vision, and the sensation I had on that quiet evening was really that of a voyager who, with youth in his heart, steers for the unknown.

The railway company had done what it could to encourage what I may term the eclipse atmosphere. On each seat were two booklets, one telling us about eclipses and the other what we were to do when we got to Richmond. Even the menus in the restaurant car had been pressed into the service of the great event: each bore upon it the proud words, "Solar Eclipse Special." The passengers, from the grizzled old men, who looked so exactly like scientists that they were probably stockbrokers, to the children being taken by their parents to see what they would never see again, were in that state of pleasant garrulity usually associated with a few drinks. Throwing aside the habitual reserve of the English, strangers exchanged optimistic weather prophecies with an eager readiness born of doubt. The train flew northwards into the night, not like an ordinary train, which is merely a commercial enterprise, but like a train freighted with a magic promise—a train whose destination was a question-mark.

We reached Richmond, nestling grey beneath its walls, in the early hours of the 29th, and by the time I emerged, about four-thirty—why indulge in the trivial illusion of summer-time when dealing with something so fixed in real time as an eclipse?—other special trains were steaming in, as if the largest beanfeast on record

were about to begin. Through the brief summer night
that little town in the fells had been awake, watching
for the dawn, and now, as the morning advanced, in-
creasing surges of people were invading it, winding
their way uphill towards the high ground beyond.

When I arrived on the moors crowds were already
scattered over them. Who can tell where they had all
come from or how they had all got there, but even on
the summits miles away one saw people in unending
droves. It seemed fitting that the race-course should be
the centre of it all, for it was just as if a race-meeting
was due to begin, the chief event of which was to be the
swift passage of the moon across the sun. People sat
about on stone dykes, ranged themselves in masses
round the town band, strolled here and there in the
aimless manner so typical of holiday-makers. Some,
with that passion for eating which overtakes the English
when they are together, were devouring pork pies and
ham sandwiches, others were buying smoked eyepieces
from hawkers, others again were reading the early
eclipse editions of the morning papers, as if to gather a
foretaste of what was yet to come. Aeroplanes droned
overhead and motorcars negotiated the moor with jerky
movements. And on every face there was a kind of
expectancy, a kind of waiting look—the visible expression of one binding thought.

It was a mild morning, but cloudy and unpromising.
As the critical moment approached, thousands of anxious

glances were turned to the sky and thousands of watches were consulted. We knew that the eclipse had commenced by the passage of time alone, for at first there was no perceptible diminution of the light. Up there in the east the moon had already started to impinge upon the sun, but for us everything was hidden behind an impenetrable blanket. With a precision, beautiful and remorseless, that grandest of all natural phenomena was taking place in complete isolation.

Then very gradually, as if under a darker cloud, the light began to lessen. But the sun was still lord of the world and the shadow of the moon had as yet but blotted out a tiny edge. Straight above me there were patches of blue, promise that later on the whole sky would clear, but it seemed too much to hope that there could be any speedy break upon the leaden east.

Too much to hope, yes—but it happened. All at once the clouds parted, and there, with the effect of rushing speed, rode the sun, with the growing shadow of the moon upon it. It appeared to be flying through the clouds, as if desperately trying to escape from the dark fungus which was now visibly eating it up. Like a hunted animal, glimpsed momentarily in its dash for cover, it seemed to dodge in and out of the mist, never for one instant losing its tearing, terrified pace.

Two minutes before totality I caught my last view of it as it vanished behind the wrack. By then it was no more than a sickle of burning light, a vast and glorious

93

new moon, fighting for its life amid the clouds and still illuminating us with its dying fires. That, perhaps, was the strangest thing of all—how, up to the very second of extinction, its beams were able to flood the air. Of course, the morning had grown much dimmer in the last few minutes, much dimmer and much colder, but so long as the faintest disc of sun remained it was discernibly day and not night. And from the hidden orb rays were pouring down over the clouds—sunset rays at five-twenty in the morning!

In those final minutes the change had become more accelerated and the whole aspect of the heavens had profoundly altered. It was no longer a gradual deepening; the darkness was crashing down in waves, as if the sky were full of groups of lights that were being turned off one after the other. An unearthly pallor began to shroud the universe, and the chill, too, was not of this earth. If in some subterranean cavern one had been ushered into a long-closed charnel vault, one might have known the same shuddering cold and twilight gloom.

And then, with a suddenness which not even all that had gone before made the less impressive, it was night. Not a normal night, not a night that brings drowsiness and sleep, but a night like an illness of the solar system, presaging disaster and the end of the world. The glory of the corona was hidden behind the clouds, and perhaps for that very reason the swift darkness was the more sinister and full of awe. A mighty hush, as at something absolutely overwhelming, had fallen upon the crowd—the thing most closely resembling it is the two-minute silence in a busy London street on Armistice Day—and everyone stood motionless, as if each felt that the order of the universe had been undermined and that the real impermanence of things, which we have foolishly come to regard as safe, had been treacherously revealed. In the ghastly blackness of that night, so muted and so icy, the music of the spheres seemed jangled and the laws of nature to be breaking down.

Somebody shouted out, "Look for the shadow!" and there, sure enough, sweeping across the earth at incredible speed, was an enormous shadow. It was as if some monstrous giant, hastening from one star to another, had thrown his momentary reflection on the earth.

Those twenty seconds were an eternity. Even the sheep upon the hills gave bleats of alarm and started to run. I stared about me and to my astonishment I perceived in the western sky, in the very opposite quarter to the sun, two glowing patches of light, one above the other, cast there, no doubt, by some trick of refraction.

And as suddenly as the light had been switched off, it was switched on again. It came as it went, wave on wave following one another in mad precipitancy. We had watched, with breathless attention, every stage of the eclipse's oncome, but the moment totality was over we all, with one accord, began to make back to the town and the railway station. To follow its departure would have been an anti-climax after those few thrilling seconds and, even had the clouds permitted it, I doubt whether many would have remained to see the end. The terror had passed, not to reappear in England for more than seventy years, and people were in no mood to dally over the details of its passing.

I got back to Richmond in due course and was soon sitting in the same restaurant car in which I had dined the night before. I ordered breakfast, but somehow I did not feel quite as certain of getting it as I had felt certain of getting dinner. The equilibrium of life no longer seemed secure and the tranquil sky above held a hidden menace. For a few moments the balanced harmony of time had appeared to rock and the very heavens to threaten us with a terrible fate.

The total eclipse which will happen in England in August, 1999, will again, I believe, be of short duration; but the one which will happen in July, 2168, will last for nearly seven and a half minutes. Will our descendants have reverted to cave-life by then and fall flat on their faces in dismay or will they be so scientific that it will teach them the last secrets of the sun? I wonder.

Queen Victoria at the Close

▽

If English authors suggest England, England obviously suggests the English Monarch. The reminiscence which follows was vividly recreated for me on account of King George's Silver Jubilee. And now that the Queen's great-grandson is King it seems more than ever to belong to the dim past. But apart from that, there was something so absolutely English in the scene, so English, that is to say, in a sense which has vanished for good and all, that this little picture has for me the value of an atmosphere as well as of a memory.

CHAPTER VI

Queen Victoria at the Close

ONE HAS TO BE MIDDLE-aged to appreciate the position which Queen Victoria occupied during the final years of her life. It was, at once, so personal and so exalted, so human and so glamourous, that it can scarcely be understood to-day unless one be old enough to recall that curious mixture of emotions which was evoked by a mental image of "The Queen."

And apart from all other significance, these two words had actually come to acquire a meaning which was almost mystical. They suggested immortality. Governments might rise and fall, dynasties might crumble, the great figures of the world might die, but the Queen went on exactly the same. No one even visualized her death and in her lifetime she was already a legend. The routine of her existence hardly varied. She lived in such complete retirement between her different castles and palaces that the crowds rarely beheld her; but everybody knew that, unchanged and vigilant, she was always there, keeping her old eyes upon events and her firm hand upon the rudder of the State.

Those were the days of Imperialism, and the Queen personified, as no one ever could again, the mingled grandeur and unity—yes, and homeliness—of the Empire on which the sun never sets. If I add "homeliness," it is because the Queen herself, despite the halo in which she moved, was profoundly simple. She had the middle-class virtues, but she was not middle-class. Nor was she aristocratic. She was regal—an indefinable thing, apparently, when one is born to it—and a law to herself. And thus, outliving every one, as it were, and impervious both to change and death, those last years of her reign exalted her into a position unique, incredible and tremendous. She had become a symbol.

I have reason to remember all this vividly, for not only was it part of the spirit of the age, but once, almost at the close of her long life, I saw her in circumstances of unfading distinctness. I was very young then, a boy at Wellington College in Berkshire, and it chanced that the old Queen's grandson, the eldest son of her daughter, Princess Beatrice, was also a pupil there. And thus it happened that on May 19th, 1900, eight months before her death, Queen Victoria came driving over from Windsor Castle to see this lad.

She thus describes the visit in her Diary:

"Started at half-past three with Arthur [the Duke

of Connaught] for Wellington College, Beatrice having preceded us. Changed horses at Bracknell. The whole way along people turned out and cheered, especially where there was an immense crowd, who came up quite close to the carriage, cheering loudly and finally singing 'God Save the Queen.' . . . Reached Wellington College at five, Colonel Legge meeting us on horseback outside the gates and Sir F. Edwards outside the College, where he presented the headmaster, Mr. Pollock [now Bishop of Norwich]. Beatrice, with Drino [the grandson, now Marquess of Carisbrooke], was also there. Went first into the Chapel, where Mr. Pollock showed us the memorial to Archbishop Benson, who was first headmaster of Wellington. Then was rolled in my chair to the Library and big dining-hall, through the cloisters, re-entered my carriage, and drove to Mr. Pollock's house, where we had tea. . . . Left again at six. All the boys were drawn up, including the volunteers, and the head boy presented a bouquet in the college colours. There was tremendous cheering as we drove off."

How prosaic it all sounds, how thick with the dust of forgotten things! And yet thirty-six years and more after the event that first and only sight of Queen Victoria, seated in her open carriage outside the great gate of Wellington, remains a vital recollection. Was it, perhaps, the romance of contrast? Very still and small, in black bonnet and black dress, she looked, for all the

CARAVANSARY AND CONVERSATION

world, like a retired housekeeper who, after years of faithful service, had been given an outing in the family landau. And yet that frail, shrunken figure, with the heavy eyes and the calm expression, was no less a personage than the Queen of England, the Empress of India, the Defender of the Faith, who, by the prestige of her rank and the passage of time, had become, beyond all question, the most famous living figure in six continents. In the sixty-three years of her reign she had grown fabulous, and there she sat within a few yards of me, perfectly collected, encased, so to speak, in the hush of her assured greatness.

She was surrounded by staring eyes, by important persons whispering to one another as to the next step, and she sat there, looking straight in front of her, completely indifferent to it all, completely aloof and completely natural. Indeed, the first impression, that of her being a retired housekeeper, soon merged into another impression, which, though utterly unlike it, did not seem altogether incompatible. She was *not* a retired housekeeper, she was grander in her simplicity than all the grandees about her, she was grand with the Divine Right of Kings, but she would have understood and sympathised with the retired housekeeper better than any of the others would have done and perhaps better than she would have understood and sympathised with them.

When the Headmaster wanted to make a presentation—I recall that the only two boys presented were the sons of Sir John French, afterwards Lord French of Ypres, who was then making a name for himself in the Boer War—he first had to whisper to the Duke of Connaught, who then whispered to Princess Beatrice, who then spoke to her Mother. The Queen would turn, a momentary smile would light up her impassive face, she would give a slight nod, and immediately, as if moved by a spring, she would regain her former attitude, her hands folded in front of her, her eyes fixed ahead, as if she had been an idol meditating on eternity.

It was very impressive and very strange. The magnificent horses, trained to the last perfection, stood proudly still, and on the box the coachman, a fat man in a kilt and a glengarry, and the footman, an Indian with a turban, sat like figures of stone. (Now that I think of it, I suppose the footman had descended by then, but as I saw him first he was beside the coachman.) There was something fantastic about that pair, something which would have made people gape and laugh in the ordinary way, so hopelessly incongruous were they to the setting of that English scene, but as it was, they appeared only to heighten the mysterious glamour of that far-flung Empire over which the little old lady, sitting there in such regal tranquillity, ruled as Queen and Empress.

How I stared at her, at the Queen of England who, while still alive, had given her name to a resounding epoch of history! To my sight she might have been a princess from a fairy tale. And, indeed, she was just as unbelievable as the princess of a fairy tale, as unbelievable and as shining with romance. In the twilight of her age and the unconscious dignity of her unapproachable position she dominated that eager throng by the mere fact of her presence. One could have heard a pin drop.

And what was she thinking of, I wonder? For more than sixty years she had seen everything, she had known everybody, and surely during these latter months of her life it must have been the past that those veiled eyes were seeing. Perhaps, in truth, she dwelt in a sort of trance. She *was* the Victorian era, and that era was drawing to its close. Already she, who never changed, must have felt change in the air. But she gave no sign: so long as she lived she would be the Queen, and so long as she was the Queen the power would not slip from her fingers.

Half a lifetime ago—and I remember it as yesterday! The relief of Mafeking, which climaxed all the hysteria of the Boer War, had occurred only two days before and the visit of the Queen seemed to take on an added meaning from that event. And it was "Queen's weather," an exquisite day of the early summer, and that, too, had its own significance. In my mind's eye I can still see the Royal carriage rolling off at a smart pace—the Queen always drove at a good fourteen miles an hour—into the deep countryside. I ran beside it as long as I could and then I watched it disappear from view. The Queen had vanished for ever.

It was not many months later that I watched her coffin pass slowly through London. But somehow the pomp of that procession, solemn and stirring though it was, did not begin to give me the thrill which had been given me by the sight of a diminutive old lady in black sitting, unguarded, in an open carriage.

European Holidays

HOLLAND
NORWAY

▽

*The old Queen, who used to be
called the Grandmother of Europe,
was related to practically every
reigning European house. Perhaps,
therefore, it is but seemly that this
chapter, which deals with two of
the few remaining European kingdoms, should be placed here. I am
glad I made these little tours and
so enlarged the horizon of my European experiences. They are
fairly extensive, though nothing
out of the way, but I doubt whether
they will be much added to. My
pre-War Europe has changed too
greatly. Greece, I admit, is again
as I knew it, but what is Greece
compared to Spain, Germany and,
in a sense, Italy?*

CHAPTER VII

European Holidays

Holland

HOLLAND IS, I SUPPOSE, THE
most compact country in Europe. In the features of
the land, one and the same in their diversity, in the
individuality of the race, so markedly of a single pattern
above minor differences, the personality of the country
emerges with an amazing clarity. I do not imply
that it is an easy personality to analyze, but simply that
it strikes one like a blow.

The people and the landscape seem to complete and
complement one another, as they did in the days of the
seventeenth century Dutch painters. When one looks at
those trim villages and waterways, the sunlight sleeping
on level fields and the whole scene impregnated by an
air of careful, long-founded prosperity, one knows that
the inhabitants, with their solid appearance and staid
manners, have in them, too, the assured security and
dignity of an existence handed down through centuries

of ordered planning. The heaviness of an accomplished
past lies over everything, but it is not a disagreeable
heaviness, because it is not dead but full of life.

It may seem incongruous after this beginning to comment on the remarkable variety of scenery in this small
kingdom. But the variety itself is in keeping with a
central personality and only makes one perceive more
vividly what an homogeneous place Holland is. It is
true that the sand dunes on the coast remind one of
England and the heath country about Het Loo of Scotland, but these are only surface reminders. All Holland, from the region of canals and bulbs to the wooded
approaches to The Hague, from the bustle of Amster-
dam to the sleepiness of Haarlem, is touched by the
same spirit, whose placid, enduring force is sensed as
powerfully as is a pungent odour.

Probably the section of Holland which is the least
penetrated by foreigners is the province of Friesland,
to the east of the Zuider Zee. It is very Dutch in a
manner ostensibly different from the western portion of
the country, and as it is little known, perhaps it may be
worth while to describe an expedition I made to its
capital, Leeuwarden, with some friends.

It began by my spending the night with them at their
house at Alphen, where the Rhine, in one of its ca-
nalized mouths, passes close to the door. It was a day
of August and the low beams of late afternoon were
spread diaphanously over the broad, green flats. I sat

for a long time on the balcony, gazing idly on this picture, while twilight, suffused and pink, began to percolate through the trees and the world to darken imperceptibly. Such an evening is pleasant to remember.

And it was especially pleasant to remember next day when I awoke to find rain pouring down in torrents. My enthusiasm was about as dampened as the atmosphere, but we did not change our plans. I am free to admit, however, that that hundred-and-fifty-mile drive to Leeuwarden, with the hood down and an icy draught on my back was anything but what I had hoped for. The streaming rain restricted one's vision no more than it restricted one's imagination.

The country soon grows desolate: it loses the neatness of western Holland and stretches away in vast plains where the population is scanty. Even trees are few, save for the double line of them that borders the road and can be seen twisting ahead for miles like a green riband. The idea of Holland as a small country is utterly lost in these regions, and that day of dank, endless motoring made me feel that it was immeasurable.

Yet desolate and bare though most of Friesland, as glimpsed from a car, appears to be, there is a small part of it which is both populous and wooded. One comes upon it suddenly, this strange contrast, and just because it is so different one is scarcely surprised to notice that everybody, man, woman and child, wears a distinctive national costume. Worn naturally in a land of no tourists, and not bait-like as on the island of Marken, it is really very picturesque. But why it should be worn at all just within these few miles is more than I can say. Possibly it is some conservative streak lingering within a special group of families. That, however, does not sound a very convincing explanation.

Leeuwarden is a typical Dutch provincial town, with old buildings and radiating canals. These last, while they charm the eye at a slight distance and create for one the very genius of the land, are decidedly less æsthetic close by. Their fall to the sea is sluggish in the extreme, and the nostrils, consequently, are assailed by smells which bear no resemblance to attar-of-roses.

After dinner we strolled out into the streets. The rain was over and a crowd of people had come forth to enjoy the clean evening air. The usual Dutch crowd; so usual and unchanging, indeed, that had their costumes been but different one might have felt that one was observing the self-same crowd that Rembrandt studied. And when we went into an hotel to drink a belated cup of coffee, there, seated in a semicircle amid the old furniture, were half a dozen elderly men, talking and smoking together as in an interior by Jan Steen.

The landlord bustled up and in halting English made himself known.

"Let me assure you," he brought out, "that my hotel is the best here. There is hot and cold water in every room."

This fact seemed to be impressive to him, for he beamed with enthusiasm.

"Hot and cold water in every room," he murmured again, as though lost in the sheer wonder of it. "When you next visit Leeuwarden you must stay here. There is hot and cold water in every room."

It sounded like the refrain of a litany.

I never felt more deeply the mellow age of Holland than I did that night, when, lying in my bed, I heard stealing upon the drowsy dark the chimes of some ancient belfry clock. In the profound stillness those soft, melodious notes, like drops of water falling into a well, stirred and died away. They were golden and antique, they disintegrated time in their evocation of things gone, they had about them the peace of finished centuries.

The next day we motored back to the coast. I have few recollections of that trip, but I do recall how we came upon a magnificent château of the Middle Ages— one of the few, presumably, that have survived the insensate fury of the Revolution—and stopped for a closer examination. Carp were swimming in the pool and some of the rooms had been preserved intact with their faded trappings. But the past here was dead and shrivelled, not alive and glowing as in the masterpieces of Vermeer or the thrilling chimes of Leeuwarden.

Norway

Studied on a map the extravagant indentation of the Norwegian coast is rather bewildering. It looks as though one would lose oneself for ever in a complexity of fjords and islands and get hopelessly entangled in a maze of wanderings. That, perhaps, is why so many people who go to Norway are content to give themselves over to the discretion of the steamship companies, who have long since discovered what it is the average person either wants, or ought to want, to see. Those conducted tours must be charming, with all trouble taken off one's shoulders in the changing scenes of day to day and with music echoing romantically over still waters in the hushed silence of land-locked bays. Moreover, it must be consoling to know how much precisely, from beginning to end, the whole thing is going to cost.

But in viewing Norway in this manner it appears to me that one is liable to miss those quainter, quieter parts where the spirit of the land is most fully revealed. In these random notes, therefore, I propose to go inland, as well as to the fjords, in an effort to catch that elusive something which makes Norway so particularly delightful during the few months of high summer.

I left Bergen and all its flaxen-haired girls by the evening train. It was really an enchanting journey, for the line twists about lakes and foaming rivers, with savage Norway towering around oblivious to the cosy

114

tameness of the clustering farmhouses and sloping little fields, where the hay is spread on hurdles like family washing hung out to dry.

As far as Voss the line rises but little, but between Voss and Finse it climbs steeply into the hills, and at Finse, itself, is over four thousand feet above sea-level. Owing to the long winters and the excessive hardness of the rock the engineering problems of its construction were almost insurmountable, but now one can enjoy the scene not only in comfort but with that exciting sense of contrast one always derives from man's conquest of nature. Snow-sheds of heavy pine logs and substantial wooden fences slanting off from the track were rather suggestive of Canada, but the Norwegian food on your plate—the "aftens" with its endless variety—and the Norwegian conversation in the car kept one's mind from superficial comparisons. The level of the trees is soon left behind in these Northern latitudes and the train crawls, panting, into wastes which, in the memory of middle-aged people, were practically unknown.

The air of Finse has that wine-like quality which one so often hears of and so seldom experiences. It gives one a faint, exquisite dizziness, a feeling of ultimate felicity; and sitting at the open hotel-window I drank it in greedily as the warm sunlight of morning flooded the room. In front lay a bleak mountain lake; farther back the Hardanger glacier glittered in serrated peaks of ice. And all about me were the hills, heaped up and tumbled as if in the very ruin of the world.

I resolved to explore the fringes of the glacier, where the ice-field is broken into strange hummocks like a frozen sea, and for that purpose hired an aged guide, whose English consisted of three phrases, "Take care," "Dangerous," "I cannot see." (At that, it beat my Norwegian.) And so this old fellow, hard-bitten and tenacious as the rock, and myself toiled over the boggy detritus of the moor and then up the crusted snow until we reached the ice. At this point it was smooth, sloping before us in an unbroken sheet, but downwards to our left and growing nearer every moment as we sidled along were the pinnacles and the crevasses. Above us a sweep of snow, beneath us the peaks and nodules and precipices. After standing for a time on a shelf between two crevasses and gazing my fill upon the aquamarine tints in the lower depths, I came to the conclusion that I had no aptitude for the life of an Arctic explorer and determined to continue up the glacier away from the danger zone. I signalled this to the guide, who was behind me, but with lively alarm written on his wrinkled face he pointed upwards and gave rapid vent to the full limit of his English vocabulary. That peaceful-looking bank, shining in the sun, was a snare of hidden crevasses. (Or was it simply that he thought he had earned his money?)

I was sorry to leave Finse, but I was almost more

sorry to leave Fossli, which is a place, I should imagine, visited by very few foreigners. From Ulvik, whose fjord is so far from the open sea that its water is only slightly brackish and which is, therefore, outside the itinerary of ships' tourists, one reaches Fossli by taking a steamer to Vik and then a motor. In the grey of the morning, all the livid colours of the fjord, the slaty rocks emerging from the water, the far mountains wreathed in mist, bear the immemorial aspect of Northern sadness in the stark beauty of a typical Norwegian scene. Vik is a mere hamlet and the road thence to Fossli is one of the most remarkable I have ever traversed. It is carved out of the edge of a precipice, and the sheer drop at one's side grows deeper at each curve. And presently the Voringfoss, a waterfall of incredible dark grandeur, comes into view, as it plunges into the abyss: a cold damp hovers over its cavernous gloom.

From the top of the gorge there opens a tract of barren upland, the plateau of the hills around which other hills rise on every quarter. Just beyond the turn of the road a small hotel, perched upon the brow of the rocks, stands above the knife-cut of the ravine. A commanding, if perilous, situation.

About a mile beyond the falls two streams, fresh from the mountains, meet in a great pool to whirl around and then pour onward united to the Voringfoss. A few gulls—which, with magpies, are almost the only birds one sees in Norway—floated on the water and in the afternoon large trout began lazily to rise. The roar of the waters seemed only to enhance the deep silence of the wilderness. Across the stream the meadows of a farm, all full of August flowers, came down to the border of the pool and, with the wooden farmhouse beyond and the bare hillside, gave to the whole picture a curiously authentic feel. I watched the old farmer of eighty pottering in and out of his house. Enquiring about him later, I was told that he had lived all his life in that appallingly inaccessible corner, where the road, itself, is but a thing of yesterday. How had he subsisted all these years, how had he surmounted the interminable winters of piled snow and ghastly cold? But the stoicism of the soil is in the Norwegian farmer's blood. He clings to his barren patches, to his mountain alps, like a stubborn plant with roots deep in the earth.

Enough of Fossli. Let me say a few words about fjords.

The Næro fjord is the show one of Norway, and as such offers a matchless target for the rhetoric of guide-book writers, who, with their singular lack of light and shade, are apt to give voice to unbridled enthusiasm on the least provocation. I was, therefore, rather prejudiced against it, though I am forced to admit that it really is very fine. It twists between beetling cliffs, thousands of feet high, which, sombre and intractable, sink clear to the water's edge. And down these cliffs waterfalls drop and crash, their volume blown into spin-drift by the wind or full like an avalanche let loose.

I could talk of other fjords, of the Hardanger and the Sogne, but to what purpose?   There is, even in their magnificence, such a colourless monotony about them that descriptive words would soon cease to have any meaning. Some are grander than others, most have their special personality, but if you have seen one you have, in a sense, seen all.

I shall, therefore, end these random jottings by tell-ing how I hired a launch at Balholm, the most northerly point I reached, to take me to Gudvangen on my first stage back to Bergen.   The crew consisted of a father and son and their English was the equal of my Nor-wegian.   Indeed, about the only word we seemed to have in common was "silt," that small fish, like a sar-dine, which abounds in the fjords.   Consequently, in order to break the tedium of the run I kept pointing down at the water and saying in a voice of triumphant astuteness, "Silt!"—to which both would reply with the kind of eagerness one answers a person not quite right in his head, "Ya, silt!" I wonder whether they thought me an idiot or a fish merchant?   Yes, it was a tedious run, that long pounding of the fjord, but it had its own charm. Low on the water, Norway had a new aspect, an aspect at once more oppressive and more real.

Celebrities Out of Setting

▽

One can hardly move about Europe without seeing celebrities—often, to be sure, accidental celebrities such as princes or politicians—and so following my European chapter, I propose to give now some glimpses of celebrities I have seen or met at one time or another in surroundings with which, as a rule, one would not usually associate them. There is, I feel, something rather attractive in this idea, for celebrities being human, are apt, in certain circumstances, to reveal a more intimate side of their character when off their guard.

CHAPTER VIII

Celebrities Out of Setting

THE FIRST FAMOUS MAN— or, rather, man to be famous—I ever met was former-President Hoover. And that was in the Mount Nelson Hotel, Cape Town, more than thirty years ago. I was a mere youth then, and though Mr. Hoover himself was only a young man, he had already a reputation as a mining engineer. In those days he was slim and silent, and if, as I suppose, politics have forced him to become more loquacious, his excessive silence even in later years, when I knew him in London, was always what struck me most about him.

Though Mr. Hoover was the first celebrity I met, the first I ever saw was Professor Lecky, once prominent as an historian and as an authority on European morals. As a boy, making a tour of the Scottish Highlands with my father, I sat behind him on a coach, and to this day I have not forgotten his fantastic and helpless appearance. He bore a marked resemblance to the photographs of Horace Greeley and was so grotesquely ugly as to be positively fascinating.

There is no call to keep to a time-sequence in a chapter of this nature, so I will skip to 1913. In that year I was staying in Shepherd's Hotel, Cairo, and other guests also staying there were old Pierpont Morgan, who was to die in Rome six weeks later, and Porfirio Diaz, who had not long since had to flee from Mexico, over which he had ruled with a firm hand for so many years.

The American financier had a number of friends with him and every morning they would start out on sight-seeing expeditions in so modest a looking car that it made one smile to think of Morgan, the Magnificent, enjoying himself so democratically. I do not know whether the mere presence of the millionaire enhanced everybody's reputation for wealth, but I do know that a Parsee jeweller, who had an office in the hotel, tried to sell me a cat's-eye for seven thousand pounds, assuring me that Mr. Morgan had bought its twin.

Diaz was then a very old man, but by no means decrepit. I caught only one glimpse of him, and that was when he was driving with his youngish wife through the Cairo streets. The companion with whom I was had an immense admiration for the ex-dictator and, seeing his chance, rushed after the carriage and, over-taking it, called out in Spanish that he was the greatest man in the world. I should suppose that Diaz must have had a moment of fright, thinking, no doubt, that here was a revengeful Mexican, but in answer to my companion's salute he smiled pleasantly and the carriage rolled on.

If Morgan and Diaz were far away from their normal settings in Cairo, Clemenceau, whom I saw at a garden party in Rangoon in 1920, seemed even farther away from his. A Frenchman usually has an air of being slightly lost when he is out of France, and it was odd to watch the grim Clemenceau behaving as meekly as a lamb on a Burmese lawn. He was accompanied by a little bearded compatriot, who looked precisely what I understood he was—a rich manufacturer or tradesman. Doubtless it was he who was footing the bill for that jaunt into the Orient.

Talk of the Orient reminds me that when, a few years later, I met Lord Haldane at dinner he affably but earnestly cross-examined me as to the prevalence of fleas in China. Now, though I have seen China, I have never set foot in it—just as I have seen Siam, Palestine, Haiti, Ireland, Albania, Uruguay and other countries where I have never landed—, so I hardly know why he should have supposed that I was an authority on that elusive subject. I presume I had been talking about some book I had been reading.

That dinner was given by the Ranee Margaret of Sarawak—alas, I have had to change her from the present to the past tense in the proofs!—who was a remarkable old lady with a strong sense of humour. I remember her telling me gleefully how, before Sarawak obtained full recognition, the Rajah used, in the Court Circular, to be put on the same footing with the head of the Salvation Army. It was, "The Queen received Sir Charles Brooke (Rajah of Sarawak)," just as it was, "The Queen received Mr. William Booth (General of the Salvation Army)." Afterwards, she added, Queen Victoria kissed her, as showing their equality as sovereigns. I also well remember the honeyed tone in which the Ranee mimicked Anatole France's voice on being presented to her—"Ah, la Reine de Borneo!," as he bowed low over her hand.

Another guest at the same dinner was Sir Edward Elgar, the composer. I recall nothing about him save that he looked just like a country squire, which, I am informed, is exactly what he wanted to look like. A very sensible wish, in my opinion. If we lived in the age of Guilds it might be seemly to dress according to one's business or profession, but as things are it is wise to be as inconspicuous as possible. I would prefer, any day, to be taken for a country squire, which is, more or less, a general term for a nonentity, than for a writer, and an obscure one at that.

The present Rajah Brooke of Sarawak was also there. He is an intelligent and rather unfathomable man, but is chiefly remarkable as being the only white rajah. He once asked me to stay with him for three months in

Sarawak: it might have been an interesting experience.

The only other rajah I ever met—and he, too, was far from his domain—was "Ranji," once so famous as a cricketer and then a portly man of about sixty and the Jam Sahib of Nawanager in western India. A publishing firm wanted me to write his Life and I saw him several times at the Hotel Metropole, where he used to put up, when in London, with a retinue of native servants. He was extremely courteous and, though rather indifferent to the scheme, asked me to stay with him in India. I was on the point of starting out when I got news of his sudden death. Things always happen like that.

Another illustrious Indian to whom I was introduced in London was Sir Rabindranath Tagore, the poet. His manner was mild and meditative, his face that of a saint, and though he was not perhaps the outstanding poet his admirers then believed him to be, he had, to perfection, that air of aloofness from worldly things which one associates with Eastern wisdom.

While on the subject of Oriental personalities, I might mention that, when he was First Secretary to the Japanese Embassy in London, I occasionally encountered Mr. Tokugawa, whose family had been the real rulers of Japan for hundreds of years. His father, Prince Tokugawa, would have been the Shogun, had not that title been abolished in 1868; and in the presence of the son, who would have succeeded in due course, one could not but be conscious how, in Japan, the mediæval and the modern are inextricably mixed. Unlike England, Japan does not merely live upon the shell of the feudal system: the feudal system interpenetrates her very being. I once discussed with Mr. Tokugawa the relative status in the body politic of the Japanese nobility and the British peerage, but I feel quite sure that I made myself no more plain to him than he did to me. It was as if two deaf people were trying to carry on a conversation.

Sir Hugh Clifford, the leading Colonial administrator of his day, asked me to stay with him both when he was Governor of Nigeria and Governor of the Straits Settlements. I wish I had been able to accept, though the life would probably have been too strenuous for me. For Sir Hugh, whom I have only seen out of his setting, is a man of the most tremendous vitality and used to begin his working day about four A.M. His books of Malayan stories are increasingly admired, and I am glad to think that he was able to fulfil what he told me was his life's ambition—end his official career as Governor of the Straits Settlements, where he had begun it over forty years before.

If Elgar looked like a country squire, so also did Lord Headley, who was distinguished as being the only living Mohammedan peer. (I think that Lord Sheffield, before him, had also been a Mohammedan; while, if my memory is correct, Lord Mexborough had been a Buddhist. Lord Sinha, an Indian, is naturally a Hindu.) He was a delightful, simple old man; so simple, indeed, that I once had the temerity to ask him why he had become a Moslem. His answer was that it was the religion which brought him peace and happiness —and what better answer could he have given? He had spent many years in India as an engineer, without any expectation of inheriting the title, and it was there, of course, that he had been brought in contact with Mohammedans. He made the Pilgrimage to Mecca, wrote a pamphlet about it, and presented me with a copy. But it was incredibly dull: in truth, had he spent a week-end in the suburbs and recorded his experiences, they could not have been more insipid.

I cannot imagine a more startling contrast to Lord Headley than was George Moore, whom I once met at the London flat of "Elizabeth"—Countess Russell. He was obviously not pleased to see me, for he had been expecting a tête-à-tête, and his tone was far from cordial. He had a sort of drooping, clammy manner, and conversation between us did not flourish. And if he had guessed that I was a friend of Conrad's he would probably have been more distant still: I am told that he had a rooted prejudice against the writings of the great Pole and could not understand why his manuscripts and first editions were more sought after than were his own.

"Elizabeth," herself, is just as witty and scintillating as her books and is, in her own line, the finest letter writer I have known. It seems to me that her work has never received sufficient recognition and that one day her literary reputation will stand higher. Katherine Mansfield, on the other hand, who was her cousin, did achieve high literary fame for a few years, and her all-too-early death was lamentable. She was a delicious creature and, like "Elizabeth," very witty. She once told a friend of mine that the cottage in which she was then living had such low ceilings that the only thing she was able to cook was pancakes.

I have met, incidentally, a good many other women writers of note, from the austere Mrs. Woolf, who has now attained a niche where "Virginia Woolf," tout court, seems a proper mode of reference, to less formidable though perhaps more lively ladies. But those meetings were invariably so haphazard and so invariably at meals that they did not leave much impression on me and, I am certain, none at all on them. Why, therefore, give a list of names? It would only be embarrassing.

I might add here that I used to know Lady Ritchie, who, apart from being one of Thackeray's two daughters—Mrs. Woolf's mother was the daughter of the other—was a writer of distinction. I believe that Edward Fitzgerald greatly admired her novels, though presumably they are unread to-day. How sad it is to contemplate all the labour that ends in oblivion! Lady Ritchie, who, in her gracious Victorianism, had about

her something of the flavour of old lavender, retained,
I believe, vivid recollections of her father.

And Tennyson's son, with whom I became slightly
acquainted in the Isle of Wight, retained even more
vivid recollections of his, although the Life of him
which he wrote is perhaps the most ponderous work of
filial piety ever produced. If only he had let himself
go occasionally and allowed us to see the racy human
being beneath the cloak of the prophet! The second
Lord Tennyson did not strike me as a particularly impressive man, although he had been Governor General of Australia; but I could never help staring eagerly
at him because, both in appearance and mannerisms, he
was the living image of a friend of mine who used to be
a railway engineer in Brazil. The resemblance between
them was, indeed, incredible and I would have given
anything to watch them together. But as they are both
no more the chance has gone.

Genius being seldom hereditary, one usually feels
more curiosity than hope in meeting the children of
geniuses. But it has been remarked before now that
the Darwin family offers an exception to this rule, and
undoubtedly Sir Francis Darwin, the only son of Charles
Darwin I knew, was a scientific botanist of advanced and
original attainments. I once stayed with him in Glou-
cestershire and was enchanted by the experiments he
showed me on the breathing of leaves. He was a de-

131

tached, amiable, easy-going man and as simple in his bearing as was his remarkable father.

The Wedgwoods, who have intermarried much with the Darwins, have also retained the forceful power and integrity of their direct ancestor, the celebrated Josiah. So many of them are close friends of mine that it is hardly for me to write about the family; but I will say this, that in character and ability, in staunchness and independence, they form a unique clan—perhaps the one real clan in England. And I am delighted to observe that the latest generation of all, the great-great-great-great-grandsons of Josiah Wedgwood, give every promise of carrying on the tradition in the most vigorous fashion.

If I met George Moore, as I have related, only once, the same is true of Arnold Bennett, although we corresponded occasionally. I went to call on him by appointment when he was staying with friends in South London and his air of poise and good sense was precisely what I would have expected. He was the very "card" he had portrayed with such gusto, assured, self-sufficient, but touched a little with the disillusionment of success and middle-age. I felt that we shared a common bond in our intense admiration for Dostoievsky and I would have liked to see him again if only to discover why it was that he placed, as I gathered from one of his later articles he did, *The Brothers*

132

Karamazov above *The Idiot* and *The Possessed*, which appear to me to be so demonstrably superior.

The enormous, the unbelievable energy of a man like Bennett makes it difficult to picture him out of his setting—at a table, pen in hand, before a sheet of paper—, but I know two other authors who are just as industrious and yet always seem to be on the go. One is Mr. E. V. Lucas and the other is Mr. Hugh Walpole. How they find time to lead the social life they do is something I can never understand. But there it is. Mr. Lucas's dry wit and Mr. Walpole's boyish enthusiasm would appear, in their different ways, to make existence boundlessly enjoyable to them both, and I suppose they take work in their stride as other men take pleasure.

Mr. Lucas, who is extremely hospitable and loves entertaining, is a first-rate judge of good food and good wine, and so, too, is Mr. Norman Douglas, whom I used to meet before the War when he was acting as assistant editor to Austin Harrison on "The English Review." Cynical, kindly and learned—he is the sort of man, for instance, who would probably know the Latin names for the different orders of beetles—he was invariably hard up and invariably cheerful. I remember that he once let me have a set of his Capri pamphlets for eighteen shillings: they became very valuable later.

Another author who had huge powers of work and huge powers of enjoyment was G. K. Chesterton, who was not only one of the most brilliant, but one of the most modest of men. It was a pleasure to talk to him; he put one on a level with himself and could appear interested even when, in all likelihood, he was not. And his wit played about his conversation just as it played about everything he wrote. The last time I met him he was wondering, with amused surprise, why it was that men who had attained a peerage should so long for another step upwards. It does not sound a very inspiring theme, but as usual he treated it with that kind of originality which nobody else quite possessed. Famous though Chesterton was, I cannot help thinking that his versatility kept people from appreciating to the full the extraordinary nature of his gifts. I do not even believe he appreciated it himself. I knew him for a long time, but saw him seldom. I wish it had been more often; his presence made one feel better in every way.

In his *Autobiography* Chesterton speaks with affection of Sir Sidney Colvin, whom I got to know towards the very close of his life. His beloved wife had recently died and nobody was allowed to sit in her empty chair by the fireplace in the drawing-room. I was unaware of this and there still rings in my ear the cry of dismay he uttered when, all-innocently, I showed signs of doing so. It was poignant and so, indeed, was his conversation, with its recurrent theme of hoping soon to join her in death. He had not to wait long for his happy release.

Colvin was a great friend of Conrad, who used to

refer to him affectionately as "Siddy," and he had also been a great friend of Robert Louis Stevenson, so that he seemed like a bridge between the old world and the new. Stevenson was, of course, before my time, but a brother-in-law of mine used to relate how he had seen him at a party in Edinburgh pretending to be tipsy when he really was tipsy. Rather a neat way of carrying it off, but obviously only possible in the early stages.

An aloof personality, in his own style, is Mr. Jacob Epstein, the sculptor. Some people, I have heard, find him difficult to get on with, especially if their opinions on art do not coincide with his, but I have invariably found him most friendly, even if a little ungetatable, and I have know him for more than twenty years. He is a man with intense feeling for his work and (though this is *not* out of setting) I can never forget the absorbed look on his face while he was modelling Conrad's head at Oswalds, the novelist's home near Canterbury.

I have not had the luck to meet Mr. H. G. Wells, but this mention of Conrad caused me to dig out and read again a postcard Mr. Wells sent me when, in 1912, my first volume of stories appeared. With the ardour of a beginner I had forwarded him a copy and with the sternness of a realist he acknowledged it in these words, "You are drunk with Conrad. You have got a style before you have got a story, and God help you." I dare say he was right, but some of the other famous authors to whom I had presented copies answered more encouragingly—Hudson even wrote, "There is a fascinating quality in all the pieces, which is entirely your own, I think," thereby seeming to controvert Mr. Wells's verdict—, though perhaps it would have been better in the long run had they not. However, I have had some good times, even if I have not acquired much reputation or made much money.

But I was talking about celebrities, not about myself. And looking back, whom do I not see?—Dr. Jameson of the "Raid" chatting to a group of friends in Cape Town; Venizelos, inscrutably calm, attending the Greek Royal Family at the Athens railway station; Lord Morley, grey and old, getting into the train after Meredith's funeral; Arthur Balfour addressing the House of Commons in his beautiful, dandified voice; W. S. Gilbert striding over his estate at Harrow with anything but a genial expression; Melba and Caruso singing together at Covent Garden in "La Bôhème" (very much in their setting, I agree); Sir Squire Bancroft strolling in the West End, as debonair and immaculate in his eighties as a peer of long lineage from the pages of Ouida; Rupert Brooke, handsome and smiling, threading his way through the tables of the Café Royal; King George V in a lounge suit and grey bowler hat, enjoying himself at the Wembley Exhibition. All dead, all snatched for an instant out of the pigeon-holes of visual memory.

And as for people I have actually met, a crowd of famous and half-famous names floats before me—

136

novelists, poets, painters, composers, critics, historians, philosophers, scientists, politicians, diplomats, judges, admirals, bishops, actors, actresses, and goodness knows who else; but I do not wish this chapter to degenerate into a mere catalogue, so I shall say little more. Certainly I once met a legginged Mr. Bernard Shaw in a barber's shop, Mr. W. B. Yeats at the house of a friend, Mr. Augustus John in a restaurant, Mr. Wilson Steer on the Embankment, muffled up to the eyes, Mr. Muirhead Bone on board ship, Mr. Bertrand Russell at Cambridge, Herr Leon Feuchtwanger at a New York luncheon, Monsieur Maurice Ravel in Chelsea, and certainly I have met, in such chance circumstances, many other of the renowned; but these are facts of no faintest significance. People reveal themselves deeply, though not always with the sudden ease which informal surroundings may induce, only to their intimates, and there is no point in boring celebrities with one's presence, praise or opinions. And in this respect, it is just as well to bear in mind that celebrities can bore as readily as be bored.

Sunlight and Darkness in Kentucky

AUTUMN DAY
NIGHT WOOD

▽

*Because the first celebrity I ever
met was a citizen of the United
States, as described in my last chapter, it does not seem unreasonable
that my first chapter about the
United States should follow here.
The place of which I write now is
known to numerous people on both
sides of the Atlantic and, though I
have mentioned no names and been
purposely rather vague, may possibly be recognized by some. The
man who was my host has friends
everywhere, but he does not seek
publicity and would, I believe, prefer not to have his retreat too
clearly indicated.*

CHAPTER IX

Sunlight and Darkness in Kentucky

Autumn Day

KENTUCKY CAN NEVER have known a more perfect day. There is not a cloud in the sky, a honeyed breath of wind stirs through the branches, and the growing warmth is interlaced by that touch of autumn which serves to round off and complete the rich fulfilment of the scene.

The farmhouse lies shining and still amid its trees and the morning sunlight casts here and there deep shadows upon its whitewashed walls. A great calm and a great hush are over all. It is as if the year, freed of its labours, were content to drowse away its respite, aware that it has completed its purpose and can be at ease awhile before the profounder sleep of winter.

The trees have just begun to turn: there is a faint suggestion of bronze upon their green and very soon now they will all be flaming. The light catches the fluttering leaves and the wood beyond the house glitters

141

and ripples like a dancing sea. The whole atmosphere is, indeed, saturated with buoyant light. The Ohio hills stand out in the clear magic of annihilated distance and everything seems to have stepped nearer. The mists have melted from the river; under the brilliant sun it resembles a narrow lake with the ruffle of a breeze mantling its long expanse. From up here it is impossible to mark its flow: all one sees is that lovely strip of colour suspended between the sloping banks of either shore. A wonderful vista, and on this day of the early fall more wonderful than ever in its illusion of eternal summer.

Let us walk out into the gathered harvest fields. The corn has been collected into stooks and the stubbled earth is dry and friable. I like to feel it thus beneath my feet, just as I like to gaze at bare fields backed by yellowing woods. Perhaps through an association of ideas the earth has a new beauty at this season. It has given up its fruits, it has finished its task, and yet there is nothing of desolation about its warm maturity. Too soon it will be an unconscious, frozen mass, but now it appears alive with the spirit of the ripened year. Even the pumpkins, swelling upon its surface, are but a symbol of all it has accomplished; henceforward it is to the sun alone that they must look for sustenance.

From the summit of the hill that skirts the wood above the near-by fields a panorama, grave and magnificent, unfolds itself. Kentucky and Ohio, divided by

142

their gleaming river, stretch all about one in a confused harmony of wooded ridges. From this vantage-ground the ample picture, so full of silence and of sunlight, has the aspect of a primeval wilderness. So must it have looked when the first settlers forced their way into this smiling land and so, assuredly, will it look a hundred years from now.

The house and farm buildings lie directly beneath, but only glimpses of them emerge through the rampart of their surrounding trees. A verdurous flood seems to be swallowing them up, even as jutting rocks are swallowed by the incoming tide. But it is such glimpses that entice imagination with the promise of welcome and enable us to enjoy without foreboding the treacherous grandeur of the waste.

A mere handful of apples still hangs from the branches and the grapevines are already withering. The Kentucky harvest is practically over, but summer lingers on. The bees are working around the hives, cicadas stridulate in the grass, butterflies waver over the flowers, and birds utter plaintive little notes, as though ready to burst into their spring song if only they dared deceive themselves. High overhead, all black against the blue of the heavens, a turkey-buzzard floats by on motionless wings, while on the garden wall a chipmunk, ceaselessly busy about its secret affairs, darts to and fro. How quickly all will change, and yet, while it lasts, how exquisite is this long-drawn pause, holding off, as it were, with passionate backward glance the approach of an inevitable future.

Large beds of flowers, whose varied colours glow more intensely as the day declines, are blooming in the garden, and on the trelliswork of the house the luminous blue and white of morning-glories and of moon-flowers has not yet been blighted by an autumn frost. It will come soon enough, that milestone of the wheeling year, but as life itself is only a succession of days, why think always of to-morrow?

I am surprised to see how fresh everything is. In the plains the drought has been very severe and crops have been hopelessly ruined, but on this sheltered hillside nature has been milder. And somehow one would expect that of this spot, where existence passes so placidly. It is curiously delightful to discover anew how truly it resembles a kind of oasis. Reality so seldown fits into the scheme of the ideal.

It is strange to hear the rattle of the Chesapeake and Ohio trains in the valley beneath. A wall of trees at the foot of the steep garden hides from my sight anything beyond an occasional puff of steam and the whole landscape is so foreign to thoughts of the outer world that the noise breaks in as an incongruous invasion. Country sounds, however loud, do but deepen the inner quiet; but an engine's whistle can disrupt the spell and bring, by suggestion, the worries of civilization into this quiet refuge.

The last rumble has died away. The valley is hushed again and the burnished river glimmers in the empty splendour of the middle distance. I have not seen a craft upon it all day, but that is only chance. There is really a considerable river traffic between Cincinnati and Pittsburgh, and on a summer evening it is a pretty sight to watch from the lawn a passenger steamer—perhaps one of those Show-Boats that still bring romance to rural lives—glide slowly by, lit up from stem to stern. Music sounds afar upon the waters, and so faintly and sweetly is it heard up here, wandering through the air like the disembodied echo of an echo, that it seems more like the pulse of the brief, dreaming night than a reminder of the realm of men.

Nowadays it is too cold to sit out late and log fires have already been started. In the noontide heat that sounds absurd, but the year pursues its destiny and one shivers as the sun goes down. The great thing is to keep hold of the light as long as one can and to taste the flavour of each individual minute. For there are subtle, ceaseless changes even in the monotonous constancy of a cloudless day, and these very changes are reflected in ourselves. The mind reacts to gradations too infinitesimal to be analyzed, and if one is never bored by natural beauty, it is because the outward face of things alters everlastingly.

I have been sitting for a time in the summer-house, which overlooks the main garden, wondering why it is that while in certain moods knowledge helps pleasure, in others it dampens it. I do not want to regard these beds of colour scientifically and would almost rather I did not know the name of a single flower in them. Is it, perhaps, that on this day snatched from the dying summer knowledge and melancholy would go hand in hand? For the name of a flower conjures up its season, and the season of all these flowers is nearly over. But regarded as colour alone they are part of the general illusion: these mortals have taken on immortality.

The regular life of the farm goes on about me, but on such a day as this one is hardly aware of it. The details appear to be merged in a serene immobility, just as a spinning top looks motionless. An odd feeling of detachment, which comes from the keener enjoyment of every sense, gives to the whole scene a visionary tinge: it is almost as though everything were encased in the silence of some ancient enchantment.

As I said in my preliminary note, I have made no effort to describe this Kentucky farm in particulars. What I have attempted to do, rather, is to create the atmosphere which permeates it on this autumn day. I am not at all sure that I have succeeded, for the creation of atmosphere is no easy matter. I will only add, therefore, that it is a place which seems to have eluded the unrest of the age, nestling there with its gardens and its woods, with its hillside slopes and spreading fields, like a secure haven that no storm can engulf.

146

Night Wood

Many a Southern farmer adds to his income during the winter months by hunting the opossum, whose pelt has an appreciable value. When nights are dark and scent lies well he ranges the woods with his trained dogs. As soon as their barking announces that a 'possum has been treed he hurries towards the sound, finds the dogs frantically scratching at one particular trunk and, swinging his lantern aloft, catches the reflection of two peering eyes. A shot or, if the tree be small, a shake, followed by a jump, a rush—and all is over.

But in September, of course, the foliage is still dense and the animal can hide, invisible, amongst the leaves. In short, it is too early for successful 'possum hunting, but nevertheless, as it was my only chance, a hunt was organized. To wear one's oldest clothes and to bring a stick were the sole instructions. It all seemed delightfully simple, and I visualized an expedition which, if it resulted in nothing else, would, at least, show me the Kentucky woods in their dim mystery.

It was a night of the Indian Summer, one of those nights that, in the clear intensity of the sky and the deep quiet all around, conveys, as does nothing else, a sense of ultimate grandeur. The feel of the earth was warm from the day and the woods above the river slept in the aromatic hush of autumn. The glow of the rising but as yet invisible moon crowned the hill and the stars

147

dwindled imperceptibly. There was not a breath of wind, not a murmur of any kind, and upon all nature there seemed to have fallen a solemn peace.

We were a party of half a dozen, together with a guide and his two dogs. Not much to look at, these dogs, being unhandsome mongrels of a deplorable vagueness, but from their whining excitement they evidently knew their job.

"Guess they'll find whatever there is," observed the guide as they dashed off, and presently, sure enough, we heard them baying in the depths of the wood. There is something primitive in all of us which responds automatically to a hunting cry; and that ominous, persistent sound, breaking the silence of the night, started us all running. Well, scrambling would be a better word, for what with the unevenness of the slope and the barriers of undergrowth we made slow work of it. Distant noises are not easy to locate precisely, especially when hearing obtains no aid from sight, and it was astonishing how soon we got separated in that dense wood and how far apart echoed our questioning shouts.

But at last we all reached the spot. The dogs were pawing at a tree-trunk or jumping into the air around it. And now and again, as if to change their tactics, they would sit down on their haunches, cease barking, and stare appealingly up at the branches. They looked quite ridiculous at such moments, with their expression seeming to say, "Do please oblige us by coming down at once." But nothing stirred up there and nothing was visible. Somewhere, motionless as the bough to which it clung, the 'possum was staring fixedly down at us, but the tree was too thick with leaves for the lantern to catch the glint of its eyes. And it was too large to shake.

"Call off the dogs and try again," said my host.

To the guide's orders away they went once more, their brief memory of frustration fired by new hope. But as for me, I sat down and began to smoke. I was not optimistic. Surely every night prowler for a mile in each direction must have taken cover by now. But what was that?—more barking? Yes, by Jove! Only this time it was a different note altogether, not triumphant but short and angry. The guide pricked up his ears.

"Reckon they've found a skunk!" he exclaimed. "Best hurry if you want to see it."

I *did* want to see it. I had heard a good deal about skunks, exaggerated things I felt, and I was anxious to meet one face to face. Occasionally motoring along a country road a friend had remarked to me, "There's been a skunk about here," and I would be conscious of the ghost of an odour, an indescribably musty odour, clinging to the atmosphere like a stain. But it had always been just that, a mere ghost, and I wanted to get to close grips with it and judge everything for myself.

And thus when the guide cried out, "You'd best hurry," I hurried. It was no simpler matter than before, but I went faster. I was not going to miss my skunk, not if I could help it. And I did *not* miss it.

In a clearing of the wood, dimly discernible in the crepuscular twilight, the two dogs, their bodies taut, their noses extended, were barking at a black-and-white animal the size of a cat. Every few seconds they would make as if to rush in, but would instead give a sudden leap backwards. If ever fear and fury were climaxed together it was in these dogs. Their vicious barks carried a note of hysteria and I am certain that there was foam on their lips. The skunk was quite silent and moved but little.

"They're working themselves up; they'll go for it presently," volunteered the guide. "I advise you to get away right quick."

Even then I was not impressed. It looked such a harmless, pretty little animal, and, lo, now that I had seen it there was no smell at all.

"Come on!" said the guide, beginning to hasten down the slope.

I followed, laughing to myself at this unnecessary fuss, when suddenly, a full hundred yards from the spot, it struck me. There is no other word vivid enough. It was like a slap in the face, the most incredibly nauseating and loathsome smell which, in an instant, seemed to fill the whole night with the very essence of corruption. Mephitic! It stifled my breath, it burned my eyes, it was as overwhelming as a spasm of intoler-

150

able physical pain. I had to cover up my mouth and nose and run like mad, wood or no wood. I could scarcely have felt more appalled had I been enveloped in the coiling fumes of some poisonous gas.

Of course, any one who has not experienced it will shrug his shoulders—travellers' yarns!—but his scepticism may be lessened when he learns that even the dogs trained to hunt skunks are violently sick when the skunk sprays them and that I, myself, had horrible dreams about it for nights afterwards. No wonder the skunk meanders with delicate daintiness along the most frequented paths; it carries with it a weapon of defence at once frightful and bizarre.

A skunk's smell, indeed, like the most moving art, surpasses all possible expectation and leaves one with an entirely new range of ideas. Other smells are bad, dreadfully bad, but a skunk's smell is inconceivable. No matter how forcibly you may be warned beforehand, a genuine whiff of skunk is a complete revelation. And it has, if one can employ the term, a kind of vile solidity, as though one were caught in a material horror.

"Good and strong!" muttered the guide, who was no novice.

I was too intent just then on holding my breath to encourage his reminiscences, but when we were well out of the wood and awaiting the rest of the party I asked him whether it could ever be worse.

"Worse! I'll say! Wait till you get it on your

clothes! Have to bury them, that's all there is to it."

I had a morbid curiosity to hear even more.

"And suppose you get it on your hands?" I asked.

"Just has to wear off. Washing's no use. Holding them in the smoke of a wood fire helps some. You get kind of accustomed to it."

The others had come up by now, but there was no further talk of hunting. Even in that remote field the air was contaminated.

"Accustomed to it?" I repeated incredulously.

"More or less. I've skinned many a one. I don't like it, but they fetch money."

He was a stoic, but when he added, "The dogs won't be fit to go near for a week or two," and I saw one of them approaching over the grass like a grey, bounding shadow, I yelled out, "Don't let that dog come this way!"

They had the laugh on me then, but I noticed that there was no enthusiasm to greet it. These dogs may have conquered, but they were not conquering heroes.

The moon was above the horizon now and her pale gleams flooded the earth. But as I trudged homewards I was not thinking how beautiful it all was, I was thinking only of the terror that walks by night.

A Remarkable Friendship: Conrad and Galsworthy

▽

I hasten to say that, though this chapter is wholly unrelated to the one that went before, nevertheless Galsworthy stayed at least once on the Kentucky farm I described and its owner was, perhaps, his greatest American friend. Thus the thought of the place led to the thought of the novelist. As for Conrad, he had corresponded with the owner. And anyhow when have I not seized an opportunity to write about Conrad, although I have often been told— once even by Mr. Joseph Hergesheimer—that I have done my own reputation as an author harm by writing so much about another. But what do I care!

CHAPTER X

A Remarkable Friendship: Conrad and Galsworthy

Joseph Conrad and John Galsworthy first met on board a sailing-ship when they were both obscure and when neither even contemplated a literary career. But through all the chances and changes of their lives, through the development of their quite different talents and personalities, and through the call of those ties and responsibilities which grew inevitably, they remained close friends till the end.

Thirty-one years of unclouded friendship would be notable in itself, but between men of creative minds—instinctive rivals, moreover, in the same field—such a record speaks of a mutual regard and tolerance that are very rare.

A legend, which not even Galsworthy's own disclaimer was able to dispel, has sprung up about their first meeting. It is generally believed that it was to

Galsworthy Conrad showed the unfinished manuscript of *Almayer's Folly* when they travelled together in the "Torrens" and that it was to his enlightened encouragement that we owe Conrad, the author. It is all nonsense. Certainly it is true that Conrad, then First Mate of the "Torrens," did show the manuscript to a passenger, but that was on the outward voyage to Australia and the passenger's name was Jacques. The voyage ended at Adelaide on January 30, 1893, and it was only on the return voyage, which began in March, that Galsworthy was a passenger. Of that experience he wrote: "On that ship he talked of life, not literature; and it is *not* true that I introduced him to the life of letters."

But myths outlast most things, and there is a poetic fitness about this myth which will make it live indefinitely. If Galsworthy could not exorcise it, I am sure I shall not be able to.

And yet the truth about their meeting is stranger in its poetic fitness than is the fiction: Galsworthy only met Conrad because he had gone to Australia in the hope of taking ship to the South Seas and meeting Robert Louis Stevenson. A curious fact, but a true one. As that hope was not fulfilled, he booked a passage as far as Cape Town in the "Torrens" and so made the acquaintance of a greater than Stevenson. Thus do the tangled threads of existence sort themselves out and, in perspective, suggest to us the hand of beneficent coincidence.

They sailed together for fifty-six days, a long time

to be thrown in one another's company in a small vessel, and it might well be argued that a friendship which, at its inception, could emerge strong from such propinquity was likely to last.

And, as I say, it did last. When Conrad talked of Galsworthy it was always as "dear Jack" and it was always, in recalling old times, with a special tenderness. And after Conrad's death I have heard Galsworthy talk of him, and in his voice, too, there was invariably that gentle, tender note we reserve for those we have loved. I have watched the two men together: Conrad so animated, with eyes glittering from under folded lids; Galsworthy so self-contained and quietly smiling. The Pole and the Englishman; the tormented genius who wrote as with blood and tears; the calm artist with his mastery over his chosen material!

But between those two writers, profoundly dissimilar in their temperaments, there existed a bond which brushed aside all barriers and was utterly without the seeds of jealousy or change. Of late years they met but seldom, for their activities were diverse and their homes lay far apart, but when they did meet it was as if they had only parted yesterday. Death alone was capable of breaking that friendship.

And yet, though they both wrote with noble amplitude about each other's books, I doubt whether they were at heart very sympathetic—I mean, sympathetic critically, as apart from personally—towards each other's work. They encouraged one another, they followed one another's careers with brotherly interest, they rejoiced in one another's triumphs; but their aims were too dissimilar to allow of full appreciation of each other's creative qualities. What they appreciated, rather, it seems to me, was the achievement as a whole and the integrity of the workmanship.

And is not that precisely what one would have expected? They stood worlds asunder in their manner of approach and in the basic structure of their imagination. It would be idle for me to deny that I consider Conrad much the greater writer, but within his limits Galsworthy, also, was a remarkable novelist. Anyhow, what I am concerned with here is friendship, not criticism, and it is to emphasize the unconquerable nature of their friendship that I lay stress on the difference between their personalities and accomplishments.

In a sense they were diametrically opposed types and one cannot properly compare them even in their fatalism. In the very order of things, it would have been improbable that either would have appreciated deeply the work of the other. The real creator is seldom strongly attracted to creations outside the boundary of his special tastes, and though Conrad and Galsworthy acknowledged, and took pride in, each other's gifts, it was not without those mental reservations which were inherent in their attitude to their art.

Their friendship, in brief, was based primarily on hu-

man affections and not on literary affinities. If neither
had ever written a book and so come to follow the same
calling, it is possible that they would have drifted apart,
as friends so often do from mere lack of opportunity;
but had fate been kind to them—as it was—they would
have remained friends wherever their paths had led.
For there was that in each which responded to something in the other or perhaps gave to the other something he needed. Friendship is not necessarily founded
on close understanding. Conrad once said to me, "I
don't understand you, but I do trust you," and if, as I
suspect, Conrad and Galsworthy were always slightly
mysterious to one another, I know that they always
trusted one another.

Being men of receptive intelligence they recognized
each other's powers; but that, after all, was a secondary
recognition. What they recognized first and last were
the charm and loyalty of each other's natures. That
was what counted. That was what made their friendship invincible. Affection being a matter of imponderable reactions, one cannot analyze it really by explana-
tory words, and therefore it is sufficient to say that that
day of March, 1893, when they first met, was one of
the luckiest days for both ever granted them by pro-
pitious fortune.

Conrad's gift for friendship, which was extraordinary, was bound up with his feeling for the past. The
oldest of all his English friends, G. F. W. Hope, was

159

one of the simplest of men, and Conrad cared dearly for him. He and I were once week-end guests together at Conrad's, and he really was as simple and kindly a man as one could wish to meet. I remember walking with him in the garden and gathering, from what he said, that Conrad rather bewildered him. I am not surprised. But other of Conrad's old friends, such as John Galsworthy, Mr. Edward Garnett, R. B. Cunninghame Graham, Sir Hugh Clifford and Sir William Rothenstein, were anything but simple—it is pleasant to think that three of them are still alive—and there is no doubt that the magnetic quality which radiated from him affected all alike.

Conrad had, indeed, more than a gift, he had a genius for friendship. He was almost the only friend I have ever had who, if he did not hear from me for some time, would write to find out if everything was well with me. And he rejoiced in doing those little things which give one such a pleasant feeling of being remembered. I recall that on three successive Christmasses he presented me with an old silver box, a gold stud with my initials on it, and a bottle of whiskey. Two of them I have to this day; the third disappeared with the utmost rapidity.

As for Galsworthy, he, too, had a genius for friendship, although the quietism of his nature, a quietism underlain by a passion for justice and a hatred of cruelty, made it, perhaps, less apparent. He was staunch and generous and in the early days of Conrad's struggle did much to ease his path in various ways. We who came later, when Conrad was already on the eve of his grand success, can never be grateful enough to those who, during the years of hardship, cheered him on and despite the indifference of the multitude, held steadily to the belief that his work would endure and his toil be not in vain.

.   .   .   .   .

I never knew Galsworthy well, but I came to know him better after Conrad's death. He was a man of high rectitude and humanity, a man of gentle manners and tolerant outlook, but he was not to be trifled with and could veil his dislikes in a calm firmness which was very final.

And he had wider interests than one might have thought from a first meeting. I remember once talking to him about a book on the Ituri forest I had read, describing to him, as well as I could, its perpetual twilight in which wander, as shadows, the okapi and the bongo, the dwarf elephant and the giant pig, and the eager way in which he said, "I must get it." I had expected a mere formal show of interest, but he exhibited something quite different.

Galsworthy was in Italy when Conrad died and he wrote me from there a moving letter about his old friend. And again, when I sent him a copy of my reminiscences of Conrad, *The Last Twelve Years of Joseph Conrad,* he wrote me another moving letter. Perhaps, in connection with that, I may be allowed to relate here an incident which will prove, better than any statement, how considerate he was. I had meant to put his letter in my own copy of the book, but through some idiotic mischance I lost it. This was distressing and I asked Galsworthy—not an easy thing to do in a note—whether he would not write me another, which I might preserve. It was a cool request, but he acceded to it at once. His second letter, dated October 19, 1928, repeats word for word, as it seems to me, the finest sentences of his first and I have it now in my copy.

Who would not value such a document, in which he says, speaking of my book: "It gave me a great, if melancholy, pleasure. There is the glow of true friendship in it, and a faithful and delicate handling of his last years, which inspires in me a warm gratitude towards you. . . . He was, indeed, fortunate in having throughout all those last years a friend so faithful and devoted as yourself, and one who has known so well how to render the essential truth and glamour of those last twelve years of his life and the pathos, the courage and the dignity of the end."

If it appears conceited of me to quote thus from his letter, I will answer that I do so now, for the first time,

because it puts, as it were, a seal upon the long friendship of those two celebrated men and allows me, while
recalling them, to be drawn for a moment into their
common orbit.

Life
in Buenos Aires

▽

Although there is no valid bond be-tween this chapter and the last, nevertheless, as will be made clear, Buenos Aires leads to Hudson, and both Conrad and Galsworthy were great admirers of Hudson's work. A thin excuse, I admit. I had hoped to write here of Rio de Janeiro as well as of Buenos Aires, for having said something in a former book about Ecuador and Peru, I would have liked to balance these descriptions by descriptions of Brazil and Argentina—or, rather, of their capitals—; but I do not feel that any words of mine would do justice to Rio harbour, and without its harbour, what is Rio?

CHAPTER XI

Life in Buenos Aires

THE APPROACH TO BUENOS Aires, across the muddy waters of the La Plata, is not distinguished and the great docks and warehouses which give you your first glimpse of the city are lacking in that kind of romance which one associates with a South American capital.

Indeed, Buenos Aires itself, despite its area and its population of over two millions, affects one, to begin with, as a rather unimpressive city. It is so flat and its central streets, with the exception of the Avenue del Mayo, are so narrow—though, for all I know, the new boulevards may have been completed by now— that it leaves upon one a negative feeling and a sense of disappointment. To gain any real idea of it as a whole it is necessary to ascend to the top of some high tower from which one may survey its white, wide density. Then in the pallor of its endless stucco, which flows into the haze of distance, it assumes a certain grandeur—the grandeur of monotony and size—, and not only grandeur but ethereality, as though it were washed for ever by an emolient, cleansing air.

Towards the outskirts the streets broaden out, and the Avenida Alvear, with its mansions on either side and its groups of statuary down the middle, is really superb. Here is where the rich live, but, of course, there are also the outskirts of the poor, tailing sordidly off into the usual dust and disorder or straggling dismally along the river's edge. There are, in truth, large areas of mean streets in Buenos Aires which, with the tragic uniformity of poverty, might have been dumped there from any of a dozen cities in different parts of the world. And this feeling is heightened by the polyglot nature of the population. One could be an Italian, or even an Englishman, in Buenos Aires and hear, if one chose, nothing but one's own language from year's end to year's end.

The Avenida Alvear leads to Palermo Park, which, in its own way, may be called one of the sights of South America. Fringed by curving lawns and outlined by palms and white statues, it stretches for miles in all directions in a rich beauty of cunning device and noble proportion. Winding roads and bridle-paths intersect it everywhere, and its wooded depths hold unexpected lakes and rose gardens. Exquisite vistas, merging into the forest, open to right and left, and it must have been designed by landscape gardeners of remarkable vision.

One could lose oneself in Palermo Park for hours, as in a glittering maze of infinite magnitude, and if the city were worthy of it, it would, indeed, be a city of palaces.

And yet I must admit that the more I saw of Buenos Aires, the more I appreciated it and the more powerfully did I feel its atmosphere. It is a defined, Argentine atmosphere, but it is not easy to describe. There is something solid, gay and mocking about it, as if its culture were dipped in the primitive spirit of the dusty campo and its civilization were built more upon scepticism than upon faith. And it has, at its typical, that kind of gorgeousness which a large woman covered with diamonds suggests. The Argentinian, with his histrionic temperament, hankers after magnificence, after something to stagger the imagination, and Buenos Aires is the most magnificent of his achievements.

Life can be highly agreeable if one has money to spend, for action and enjoyment are in the very air of the place. The inhabitants have good manners and are punctilious socially; the restaurants, though expensive, are excellent; and there is always plenty going on. It was intensely hot during my stay, but that did not appear to slow down the pace. Buenos Aires seems to be a city made for pleasure, rather as Paris used to be—Paris the goal of Argentine millionaires!—but the seeming is probably due to the eager, hungry vitality of the populace. They live recklessly; they adore high-powered cars, swift horses, prodigal love-making.

Of recent years sport and athletics have taken a tremendous hold on Argentina, and a young man now endeavours to excel in such games as polo, golf and football and in feats of physical prowess. And nearly everybody seems to be an enthusiastic gambler. Not only do the men bet heavily on the races which take place at Palermo on every Sunday and holiday throughout the year and waste hours at the dice game of bidou, but their whole attitude is really that of gamblers. One feels that all, according to their means, would like to emulate the Argentinian of fiction—and not altogether of fiction—whose aim it is to spend his fabulous wealth in fantastic extravagances. But despite this, the average Argentinian is astute and hard-working and knows what is best for himself and for his country. Possibly the contradiction may be reconciled by saying that he is a fatalist, though as general ideas are not popular in Argentina, perhaps few of the people concerned are even aware of it.

I mentioned above the weekly races at Palermo and naturally I attended one of the meetings. A lively scene, with the President in a straw hat conversing amiably and everybody imbued with that race-meeting excitement which is the same on every race-course of the globe. Just the same. I have watched horse-racing in five continents—never with much gratification, I may add—and at every place the behaviour of the crowds was precisely alike. Indeed, crowd-psychology is amazingly plastic and will run into any mould as readily as white-hot metal. That is what makes propaganda more deadly, in the long run, than bullets.

The Buenos Aires race-course has a lovely background of high trees, and bears, I should imagine, a distinct resemblance to Goodwood. Had I looked about me casually I might have thought myself in England. But that happens so often; one country frequently recalls another. The strangest example that ever came my way was, so to speak, a double example. One spring I was staying with friends in Virginia and went to the village fruit and flower show. Later that year I was staying with friends in Somerset and went to the village fruit and flower show there. Well, in Virginia I felt as if I were in England and in England I felt as if I were in Virginia. The people, the whole tone, the very smell of the tent, so hot and stifling, were as alike, in all essentials, as two peas. Even the settings, though externally different, could have been interchanged without incongruity. It was a curious experience.

Both the men and the women of Buenos Aires dress smartly. They would rather, I have been assured, deprive themselves of proper food than forego new clothes, and an Argentine clerk, with a few hundred pesos a month and a wife and family to support, will somehow manage to turn himself out better than his English employer. But it must be remembered that if a man is to make a hit with a girl in Buenos Aires—

which is, outwardly at least, a sophisticated city—he has to be sprightly in manner and polished in appearance. That, no doubt, explains much.

There are all sorts of local customs. If you want to attract the attention of a waiter or a taxi-cab driver you hiss like a snake, while there are many complicated gestures with your fingers to denote your feelings of contempt or pleasure. You can be arrested for walking about the streets without your jacket on, but more serious moral lapses go unregarded. This is not a prudish city and so long as you obey the usually reasonable police regulations you are left very much to your own devices and can participate, if you wish, in the full tide of gaiety.

Talking of police regulations, rather an odd thing occurred one day, which brought home clearly to me the power of those unseen influences which regulate life everywhere. I was motoring toward the outskirts with some reckless young men, whose principal idea of recreation was to go as fast as possible. And we were going very fast indeed, far too fast for my liking, when we perceived that we were being followed by a traffic policeman on a motor bicycle. Now, speeding is a serious offence in Buenos Aires and if one is caught, everybody in the car, including harmless passengers, is extremely liable to be imprisoned—and from what I saw of a Buenos Aires prison, that must be a horrible experience. But my friends, instead of slowing up, went faster than ever, with the result that the policeman went faster still, eventually overhauled us, and made us stop. The youths were not at all perturbed; one of them produced a badge of membership of a famous motoring club or association in Buenos Aires and the policeman, who hitherto had looked as black as thunder, at once gave a polite salute and allowed us to proceed without further molestation. Singular thing to happen in a Republic which is so very republican.

Yes, Buenos Aires is an exhilarating place, a place of volcanic energy, and wherever one be, life flows swiftly by. But it would soon wear me out. Very soon. It would be like living perpetually at an altitude of seven thousand feet.

When I was there a British Exhibition was being held—the first all-British Exhibition ever held, I believe, outside the Empire—and it certainly did give one a queer sensation to come upon a Tudor village in this alien setting. And really it was very well done, though I am afraid that the Depression was already too firmly in the saddle for it to achieve the results in increased trade which had been hoped for. But in other directions it was a distinct success, and in the evenings the Exhibition grounds were packed with the shopkeeper type of Argentinian bringing his wife or sweetheart or daughter to enjoy the novel spectacle.

The Prince of Wales, afterwards King Edward VIII, opened it on one of those scorching afternoons when the mere sight of a man in a cutaway coat and a silk hat is enough to make one feel prickly. But not only the Prince and his brother, but the President of the Republic, the whole of the Cabinet and all the more important British residents were so attired. After all, it was an affair of international significance, and such affairs, sun or no sun, must be conducted with the decorum of usage.

The Prince began his speech in English and then, turning round to face the President, continued in what appeared to me very fluent Spanish. It was a tactful gesture, and again, when the President had made *his* speech, he made another tactful gesture by rising and shaking him warmly by the hand. Such touches mean a good deal to the formality-loving South Americans and "S. A. R. el Principe de Galles," as he was named on the police permit which enabled one to approach him, helped to cement that old friendship which Argentina feels for England. Not that the Argentinians have, as a nation, any particular regard for foreigners, but that they would probably put the English first. With them, as with other people, friendship is largely bound up with trade.

To get that police permit, as also a "Cedula de Identidad," which is a very desirable thing to have, seemed to present almost insurmountable difficulties in delay, and had it not been for a most obliging fellow-countryman with local influence I doubt whether I would have obtained the first in time to be present at the opening of the Exhibition and the second before I was ready to leave the country. Of all muddled places, where haste is of no consequence and talk avails nothing, give me Police Headquarters in Buenos Aires. But perhaps the visit of the two Princes had put them out of their stride.

I met that Englishman by chance, and it is astonishing, as I look back, how many other people of all types I met during my few weeks' stay. Those of whom I saw most, I think, were the American Ambassador and his wife, to whom I had an introduction, and the men at the cable office. Both groups were as kind as they could be, and I used to vary the hospitality of the Embassy with the hospitality of the bachelor establishment where the unmarried cable employees dwelt. The first was of a splendid nature, for the Blisses entertained in great style and had a charming way of making one feel welcome, but the second was equally enjoyable in the friendly, English atmosphere which surrounded one. But why young men, whose salaries must have been rather exiguous, should have insisted on various English delicacies instead of living off the country entirely was something I never quite understood. Perhaps it was due to a sort of nostalgia, but even so I would think many times before paying the equivalent of seven and sixpence for an ordinary bottle of Worcester sauce. However, it would be ungrateful, if only in memory, to look a gift-horse in the mouth.

Talking of Embassies, it struck me as very short-sighted of the British Government to house their Ambassador in a building precisely like a seedy suburban villa in a hideous style of mid-Victorian architecture, while the American Ambassador was housed in a stately and ample mansion. Of course, much may have happened in six years and possibly there is a new British Embassy by now in Buenos Aires. I hope so. The Argentinians are impressed by grandeur, and the British Embassy of my time was a remarkably poor advertisement for national prestige.

To catch the inner spirit of a town there is nothing like sitting in a café and watching the people come and go. I spent a fair amount of my time thus profitably and pleasantly employed—why, even in any of the countless bars, with their look of stale dissipation, one could get a succulent dish of pulchero and a bottle of admirable Chilean wine—and I found the changing, animated scene very entertaining. But unless it be in the more accepted, fashionable restaurants one does not see many women of the upper classes, though they are full of swarthy, short, rather handsome men. The Spanish system prevails and girls are closely guarded, while men can do pretty well as they like without incurring adverse criticism. At least, not publicly, though at home the women, as in all Latin countries, wield much underground authority. But they have clear, logical minds, and if their husbands want to frequent

176

bars, dancing halls and suchlike dubious places, they do not make a scene. It is only an interlude.

But how can one know much of a race or of a city after a few weeks? The vast web of Buenos Aires conceals an untold number of secrets; and at night, especially, when shadowy figures steal by you and lamps gleam behind drawn curtains, one is conscious of mystery. The darkness throbs hotly about you and mingled sounds hover upon the air. There is a sudden cry, a sudden silence, and all at once you perceive that if you were to live here for ten years you would still lack the golden key which would unlock for you the complex, hidden personality of Buenos Aires.

Watching Birds
With Hudson

▽

*These recollections of W. H. Hud-
son may fittingly come here after
my chapter on Buenos Aires. For
on the outskirts of that city—yes,
now on the very outskirts, though
formerly in deep country—there
still exists the old farmhouse where
he lived as a child. His name
stands high in Buenos'Aires to-day;
during his lifetime it was unknown.
In English-speaking countries, on
the contrary, his work is neglected
at the moment—that inevitable reaction which follows on death—, but
being great of its kind, it will endure the test of time.*

CHAPTER XII

Watching Birds With Hudson

Edward Thomas, the English poet and essayist of the countryside, whose death in the War was a real loss to letters, once told me that he believed I was the only person whom W. H. Hudson had ever asked to join him when he was on one of his bird-watching expeditions. I dare say this was a bit of an exaggeration, but it is certain that Hudson did need solitude and silence to find that sort of harmony which is the underlying texture of his books.

That is to say, he needed it when he was in the country. In London he was rather a sociable man and once a week he and his wife—a strange and fearsome old lady who, however, could unbend somewhat grimly to those she liked—used to hold an afternoon reception in their house in St. Luke's Road, Notting Hill. Then, indeed, he enjoyed meeting people, enjoyed talking about literature and especially modern poetry, and showed a sub-acid amusement at the general pageant of life. But once away from London he wanted, above all, to be by himself.

For it was in the country that peace descended upon him, and it was peace of a kind that would have been curdled into unrest by human companionship. Far from the haunts of men lay the true world of his desire. To be alone with nature was his escape, his anodyne, the secret citadel of his heart, and no one must intrude upon his rapturous solitude. This, I am very sure, was his creed. Why, therefore, he should have suggested my joining him on this one occasion and thus break the fixed habit of a lifetime must remain a riddle. Certainly we got on easily together and certainly I shared, in my own way, his interest in ornithology, but that explanation is not sufficient. Perhaps it was just one of those momentary impulses to which we are all more or less liable and which we so often regret. I cannot say; I only know that it astonished me.

I remember Conrad once remarking to me in his joking manner, "If I were a beastly bird, Hudson would take more interest in me than he does," and in a sense he hit the nail on the head. Hudson was really fond of his friends, but it was to birds and to nature at large that he gave his passionate devotion—a devotion which, not being primarily sentimental or anthropomorphic, is exceedingly difficult to define satisfactorily.

And so, I repeat, I was immensely surprised at the invitation. It came, I fancy, when we were lunching in

182

a restaurant called the Mont Blanc in Gerrard Street on an autumn day of 1912. At that period Hudson, when in London, went almost invariably to this place of a Thursday with the idea of meeting literary acquaintances. Those weekly luncheons, originated by Mr. Edward Garnett, drew many celebrities together. People turned up or not as the opportunity offered, and on different occasions I have met there such men as Conrad and Hudson, Mr. Norman Douglas and Stephen Reynolds, Mr. W. H. Davies and Perceval Gibbon, Mr. Edward Garnett and Edward Thomas. And there were many others whom I have forgotten, some of them famous, no doubt, others as obscure as was I myself.

On the particular day I have in mind Hudson, who was talking about his forthcoming visit to Wells-next-the-Sea in Norfolk, where he used to go every November to watch the wild geese, just back in England from their northern homes, turned to me with the question, "Why don't you come down too?" I did not let my astonishment show as I answered at once that I would be delighted to come. Watching birds with Hudson! Dash it all, who would have missed such an adventure!

And so it was arranged. He was to travel down on such and such a day and I was to follow a little later.

His tall, gaunt figure was the first thing I saw as I stepped from the train. He had procured rooms in a cottage near the shore and there we spent the few days that I remained with him. They were very few;

frankly, they were fewer than I had first intended. But, then, the discovery which I presently made was rather a disconcerting one. It was, indeed! Before my arrival Hudson had already regretted his invitation and his nerves were on edge at the mere thought of anybody being with him.

It was not that he said anything, it was just that it was obvious. It screamed at one. But if it was rather distressing, it had its humorous side. And, too, it was oddly fascinating to find another Hudson altogether from the one I had known, an aloof stranger absorbed, as it were, in a world to which I had not the password. Why, it was as if the dark side of the moon had suddenly revealed itself! All the company *this* Hudson needed was the cry of the wild geese, the sound of the wind along the sands, the sight of the crested grebes in the pool behind the dunes. Truly an unknown, inaccessible Hudson, to whom the presence of a human being was a mere annoyance, a mere jar upon his still contemplation of the wilderness.

I cannot say that the discovery added to my comfort, but, at any rate, it *was* a discovery. Had I never made it, I might never have appreciated to the full why it is that in so much of Hudson's writing one hears that double note of yearning beauty and of high disdain. Hudson's feeling for nature was constantly being outraged by the vandalism of mankind, and in this particular case I, the unwitting violator of his privacy, was getting the backwash of his irritation. The only thing to do was to leave him alone as much as possible and allow him to commune with his inner thoughts. It was embarrassing, but there was nothing else for it.

Hudson was then working on his book, *Adventures among Birds*—it contains several chapters about Wells and the district—and I can see him now sitting opposite me at the table of our joint sitting-room. Hour after hour he would write with steady concentration, only pausing to look up his notes or to incorporate matter that was already finished. The apparent ease with which he worked struck me as being absolutely fitting, for how could one regard the exquisite clarity of his style as anything but a gift straight from the gods? It was Conrad—to quote him again—who said that Hudson wrote as the grass grows, and to watch him at work was to make one perceive how the fine justice of that criticism had its counterpart in the very method of his composition. His hand moved with an effortless flow and upon his countenance there settled a sort of calm serenity.

It was in the mornings that he worked. In the afternoons we would go forth together, wandering over the vast saltings—runnelled sands of seventeen thousand acres, covered twice yearly by the tide—or amid the pine woods or by the Holkham meadows. Hudson always carried field-glasses, and when he was observing birds at a distance he would stand motionless with them to his eyes, as if he had been one of his gauchos shading his sight on the great pampas of the Argentine. Or rather, perhaps, an Indian of the American plains.

Many people have remarked on the hawk-like expression of Hudson's face, but to me it was Indian. To see him in the dusk, solitary by a tree, still as an image and with all his senses on the alert, suggested more than anything else a listening Red Indian of the olden days.

A mere naturalist's curiosity soon bored Hudson and a dead bird had little meaning for him. I well recall the mingled look of indifference and indignation —a suppressed indignation hidden under an air of indifference—with which he glanced at a wild goose shot on the saltings by a fowler. The proud life was gone, taken so heedlessly, and all that remained was a bundle of feathers. Never again would it utter its triumphant call, never again would it outwit its enemy, man.

Expert ornithologist though he was, Hudson could be violently impatient with his fellow experts who concerned themselves only with the dry details of the subject. Classification was all very well, but what he wanted was to feel the life and to share, spiritually, in the freedom and joy of winged existence. Moreover, ornithologists were liable to be collectors, and to Hudson collectors were a hateful breed. He could not even bear to see a caged bird, and what he particularly admired about the wild geese at Wells was their crafty vigilance in forestalling human designs upon them.

They slept far out on the saltings, surrounded by their sentinels, and it was good to hear them in the black of early morning honk to one another as they flew, invisible, overhead to their inland feeding-grounds. There they would remain all day, unapproachably on the alert, till in the late afternoon they would return, stringing across the sky, to settle for the night on the distant sands. It was a wonderful spectacle.

I recall to mind especially one of those rare November evenings, hushed and cloudless, on which all the geese, to the number, Hudson estimated, of four thousand, converged together, as by some prearranged signal, and proceeded to execute marvellous aerial gyrations and manœuvres. The world was filled with their exultant cries, and in that twilight glow they were like a heavenly host uttering their martial music above the earth. For a long time we watched them, Hudson and I, and in his gaze, I can assure you, there was nothing of indifference or indignation.

Hudson's senses responded instinctively to the varying aspects of nature. He drew inspiration from her every change, and if he rejoiced when she rejoiced, he was equally subject to her moods of pensiveness and melancholy. I mention this because, with the glorious evening of the wild geese in my mind, another evening comes back to me, a clouded, sombre evening, when we stood silently together by a dim mere as night approached.

Shy water birds were dodging in and out of the rushes and in the wood behind a carrion crow uttered its harsh and ominous croak. The very air seemed heavy with disaster. And as though in response to that lowering scene, Hudson drew more and more in upon himself, as if a deeper stillness had fallen on his soul. And yet at that moment one had the feeling that he was very close to it all and that strange hints of felicity were coursing through his veins. Indeed, those who read his books are aware how subtle were his perceptions and how, even when his language is clearest, there is the suggestion of a mystical background. It is that, in particular, which differentiates him from nearly all other nature writers and gives him a place, not alone with the great artists, but with the great seers.

Hudson was then about seventy, but he had the stamina of a young man. He could walk for hours, saying little but missing nothing, and his brain never lost its swift alertness. His was an everlastingly interesting mind, partly because it was incalculable and partly because of the character behind it. Genius is rare but real character is almost rarer, and I do not suppose that anybody ever had a stronger or more self-contained character than Hudson. He was unswervingly true to himself on all occasions and entirely free

188

from any hint of pose or moral cowardice. He went on his way, unconcerned by neglect or opposition, and if people did not agree with him it was all the same. I do not mean that he would not enter into an argument, for he decidedly would, but that once his opinions were formed nothing could influence him. He had known bitter poverty, complete neglect, and when fame and fortune came to him at last he was quite unmoved. If he had awakened to find them a dream he would simply have shrugged his shoulders. That is literally true. I remember an old friend of his telling me how she had called on Hudson once and how he had shown her, with indifference, a cheque for eight thousand pounds which he had just received from a publisher. Indeed, I am not sure that he even showed it to her and that it was not she who, seeing it lying on the table, had exclaimed at its size, only to get a half-contemptuous reply.

Well, as I have already stated without any equivocation, I quickly discovered that my presence was only a torment to poor Hudson. He was morose and fidgety and he made me aware—inadvertently, I am sure, for he had excellent manners when not too exasperated—that the visit was a mistake. I came between him and his birds, I brought the gross atmosphere of towns into his rural retreat.

And so after a few days I packed my bag and departed. One might call it a sort of flight. But even if I had failed, I had had my adventure. Oh yes, I had had my adventure right enough! I had watched birds with Hudson and, according to my friend, Thomas, no one else had ever been asked to do that. And I imagine that after that experience no one else ever *was* asked. Of course, I am not overlooking the possibility that it may have been *my* company, rather than company in general. . . . But really I do not believe it. I certainly hope that it was just one of those things which could not be helped.

My last sight of Hudson in the country was, like my first, from the window of a railway train. As I moved out of the station he was already on his way back to his beloved desolations, where he could observe the red-shanks and the curlews and the pink-footed grey geese to his heart's content, free from the maddening proximity of a fellow man. And as the short afternoon wore through and light decreased I pictured him far out on the saltings, a lone figure blending into the universal gloom and seemingly an integral part of the tragic landscape. And picturing him thus, I knew that he was at peace.

When next I met Hudson in London he was his own cordial self. Just the same, without a trace of difference: inquisitive about people, sarcastic at the expense of things he disliked, charming in his guarded frankness. But he did not refer to the visit, save casually, and I am sure that I did not. The cloak was on once more,

190

the real personality was concealed, and though I remained on the friendliest terms with him till his death,
ten years later, I was conscious that I should see him
again in no other guise.

.　　.　　.　　.　　.

This reminiscence of Hudson ends here, but the
mention of his death induces me to add a few lines.
Nobody, I am sure, ever had a greater hunger for life
than Hudson. It was his own thoughts he put into the
mouth of Richard Lamb, the hero of *The Purple Land,*
when he made him say, "What soul in this wonderful
various world would wish to depart before ninety! The
dark as well as the light, its sweet and its bitter, make
me love it."

This attitude never changed and to the very close the
thought of leaving all the fairness of the earth was
hateful to him. I remember writing to him in the early
part of 1916 to tell him of an old gentleman, recently
dead, one of whose last pleasures had been the reading
of *A Shepherd's Life,* and how he answered me that
another old gentleman, also recently dead, had been
reading the same book with interest before *he* died,
adding: "After that I ought to be able to say, 'Now
lettest thy servant,' etc., etc.—, but I can't. I hate the
thought of it as much now as when I was a boy—when
this visible world looked a very wonderful and beautiful
place to spend an eternity in."

Again, writing to me in March, 1920, he said: "I don't think I did anything before that age [thirty-seven], and I feel ten times more interested in life and its problems and wonders than I did then. If I could count on another fifty years, or, say, a hundred, I should be happy."

This steadfast delight in existence as he grew older gives one a measure of his passionate vitality. Death coming to him in his sleep came mercifully, but though he was already eighty-one years of age, it is sad that it could not have stayed its hand a little longer.

He knew that he was doomed, but bitterly though he resented the thought of annihilation, he did not flinch. Indeed, he was surprised that he had lived as long as he had. The weakness of his heart dated, apparently, from 1914. In a letter to me of June that year he wrote: "I had a bad illness in March last . . . which nearly carried me off. This has left me with a weakened heart." In another letter of October, 1920, he wrote: "My health is, of course, always bad, and it is a perpetual wonder to me that I have lasted so long." While in the very last letter I ever received from him, July, 1921, he wrote: "I have been lately down to Worthing, and must go soon again to settle my wife's grave [she had recently died]—which will be mine, too, I daresay, before long."

And yet, prepared though all his friends were for his death, there was something almost unbelievable about it. He was so intensely alive that, in the very solitude of his inner nature—he did not, I think, put up barriers, the barriers were simply part of him—one sensed a tremendous power. His quietness was like the silence of a great tide and the seal of his personality is impressed for ever upon those who knew him.

Venezuelan Sport

SHOOTING ON A LAKE
FISHING OFF THE COAST

▽

Although Hudson had a horror of sport, nevertheless the lake of which I write in the first part of this chapter would have fascinated him with its bird life, and I think I do right, therefore, in printing this chapter here. For though it deals ostensibly with sport in Venezuela, its real purpose is to give a feeling of outdoor life in its finest manifestations. It is the sportsman's privilege not merely to hunt wild and rare animals and fish, but to see wild and rare places, and I can say truthfully that no surroundings save those of Scotland and Rhodesia have so stirred my sportsman's imagination as have those of Venezuela.

CHAPTER XIII

Venezuelan Sport

Shooting on a Lake

IN THE REMOTER PARTS OF Venezuela, the swamps of the Orinoco, the tropic jungles, and the vast llanos of the south, the hunter can find jaguar, anaconda and other ferocious animals. But few visitors to Venezuela have the chance of making such expeditions and my object here is to describe some of the sport that may be obtained within a reasonable distance of Caracas.

One may range the coastal hills for deer or wait for flighting doves in the outer plantations, but for the sheer joy of outing and delight of every sense, it is surely true that duck-shooting on the lake of Valencia is the finest sport that civilized Venezuela can offer.

The day was just breaking as we left Maracay for our thirty-five-mile drive to the southern shore. Morning twilight, with its cool, fresh stillness, lay over the earth. A few carts creaked wearily along the road, cattle were already feeding in the grass, and here and there groups of black vultures hopped about some decaying morsel.

Gradually we left the plains behind and began to ascend the ridge, twisting up and up, passing through woods and by precipitous banks, climbing out of the ranch-lands so soon to be enveloped in the blistering heat of Maracay. To me, at least, there was a sensation of escape about that drive, a sensation which is perhaps never absent when one is setting forth for new places; and then, when we reached the summit, the escape was suddenly complete.

A new world lay before us, a world of unimaginable splendour, a shining, immense vista of land melting into water and water melting into haze. Beneath us the country fell away, shelf on shelf, to a plain dotted with clumps of trees and fields of sugar, and in the middle distance the lake of Valencia, green as a shoaling sea under the sunlight, spread to an horizon of purple hills, its wooded islets seeming to float upon its surface and its shores to be leaning upon the mirror that reflected them.

The spacious harmony, the supreme loveliness of that view, were like the revelation of a secret ideal. In the hush of morning the whole landscape glowed with inward fire; one almost expected to hear a strain of music, as if the spirit of beauty itself were breathing about one. And in that softness there was an illusion

198

of fragility: it was too exquisite to be real; as the day advanced it would inevitably fade away.

The winding road led us rapidly downhill, and in due course we came to a village whence starts a three-mile tramway to the lakeside. It was a typical village of low houses, inhabited mainly by peons and half-breeds, and we went into the store to buy food. Picturesque, no doubt, but filthily dirty. When I observed an enormous, hairy spider sitting on a tin devouring a cockroach, my appetite vanished and I retired forthwith.

The venerable white nag that pulled the trolley was the most wretched-looking animal I have ever seen. Its utter dejection in repose resembled the pictures which advertise homes for worn-out horses, and it was all the more surprising, therefore, when it began to canter with considerable vehemence. Indeed, it was no easy job to keep one's balance on that rickety trolley, and it was a decided relief when we came spinning safely down to the shore.

From a different angle the lake is just as enticing close by as far away. High rushes clothe its margin and a thick carpet of water-weeds stretches out for fifty or a hundred yards. On this carpet there moved, or stood rigidly still, a whole aviary of exotic birds, great herons, white egrets, waders, waterfowl—it was like one of those fanciful pictures in a natural history book which purports to show all the animals of a district in a set piece. Bright-coloured little birds fluttered about the reeds, a flock of parroquets flew screaming above them, the lake was alive with duck, and now and then strange hawks or stranger gulls would float overhead.

Two methods of duck-shooting are employed. One is to be rowed along the edge of the lake in a boat, the other is to hide in a blind at the tip of a small promontory. The first, though esteemed locally, is really hopeless, as the duck invariably sheer off out of range. But it has this to commend it, that the men beating the reeds sometimes drive a peccary (the South American relation of the wild pig) into the water. It did not happen on the day I was there, but when it does happen it must compensate for much.

The other method, however, yields satisfactory results. The duck of Valencia, a non-migratory bird of brown-black plumage, is a fowl of sociable instincts and fixed habits. In skeined phalanxes these duck delight to fly up and down the lake, and the promontory is directly below one of their air routes. Centuries of comparative immunity have made them foolhardy and the sound of shots does not discourage them. They offer easy targets as they skim by, and a couple of guns in the blind should find little difficulty in making a bag of fifty in an hour.

But even if one be shooting from the land, one must have a boat. The lake abounds in a small variety of alligator, which grows to a length of some seven feet and is called a baba. Few wounded duck escape them if left to their fate for more than a minute or two. And as one rows about, the ugly, motionless heads of babas are a common sight. When shot at, no matter how close the range, they disappear in a flash, and though one may surmise optimistically as to the outcome, the baba offers no proof.

Every moment the day was getting hotter and the sun beat down more fiercely on the smooth surface of the water. (How very different from that day when I nearly froze to death shooting duck in a boat off the New Jersey shore!) We had a drive before us of well over a hundred miles, and though the road to Caracas is superbly engineered, yet one cannot go fast over a mountain range. So we gathered up our spoils and departed, and after a brief rest at Maracay set forth for the capital.

That drive in the dusk and dark rounded off the experience on a note of magnificent fitness. As the summit is approached, some four thousand feet above Maracay, the country takes on increasingly the look of a primeval wilderness. Range after range of derelict hills stretches before one and the track hangs upon the edge of the abyss. Everything is on a scale of terrifying vastness. Even the moon, rising blood-red and full beyond the farthest barrier, appeared enormously enlarged —an effect, doubtless, of refraction—whilst the very vagueness of the night seemed only to suggest immenser horizons. Scrub fires, like gigantic serpents whose poison shone through their skin, crept snakily upon the mountain slopes and the chill of desolation was in the air.

And thus, with the ducks fastened outside the car to keep them fresh, we came to Caracas in time for supper.

Fishing off the Coast

The coast of Venezuela is steep and wild. A port like La Guaira, huddled directly beneath the mountains, is a rare oasis in that arid region, and some miles to the westward the country is utterly uninhabited save for a few primitive fishing villages. But though the shore be barren, the sea is rich, and the finest fishing imaginable is to be had within a few hundred yards of the land.

But even if there was nothing to catch, the expedition would be worth making for itself alone. The road from Caracas to La Guaira sweeps grandly down the coastal range, and the first sight of the sea, lying in glittering and measureless expanse beneath, is enough to take one's breath away. To view one's goal afar in the very fullness of its beauty is already to feel the taste of victory.

The afternoon was calm, and as we approached nearer and nearer the faintest speckle of white foam was visible on the surface of the water. Turning off from

202

the main road into a sandy track between cactus bushes, we arrived at the appointed place where the motor-boat was to meet us.

There she was, riding at anchor in the bay. A ground-swell heaves for ever off the Venezuelan coast, and it was no easy matter to launch the canoe, which, in several journeys, took us and our supplies on board. But at length all was accomplished and preparations to fish were at once begun.

They were rather elaborate. A kind of harness is strapped to one's back and hooks from it are fitted into rings on the upper edge of the reel of the tarpon rod, while the rod itself is placed loosely in a socket clamped on to the seat between one's knees. Thus you are given sufficient purchase and support to play a great fish, fighting for its life, at the end of several hundred feet of line.

And you need it. A red snapper, carete, pargo or barracuda—that terrible fish with teeth like razor-blades and a taste for human flesh—will carry away your line, with a brake so strong upon it that you can scarcely pull it out yourself, in a rush, and it is all you can do to keep any control over the reel. And when it comes to winding in such a fish, never daring to relax the strain for an instant, you are positively "blown" by the time its flashing body looms alongside.

The motor-boat patrols up and down the coast at just sufficient speed to give the spoon bait the realistic appearance of a swimming fish. And quite evidently the deception is admirable, for the ravenous monsters which hover in wait down there, as in a ghastly game of catch-as-catch-can, never seem to doubt beforehand that they know what they are doing.

Long, lean fish and squat, deep-bellied fish were equally deceived, and so even was the tarpon, the greatest and the gamest fish of them all, which proves that a tarpon, if suitably beguiled and sufficiently hungry, has, like lesser fish, its moments of reckless folly.

It was late in the afternoon when the first tarpon was hooked, and the empty coast echoed to our shouts as the silvery form leapt into the air astern. To watch a tarpon being played is really exciting. A courageous fury seems to seize upon it the moment it feels the hook in its mouth. It jumps straight out of the water, twisting on itself and shaking its whole body, and until it be free or worn out it continues so to jump, as though galvanized by a proud strength and resolution. So game and crafty is the tarpon that it usually succeeds in ridding itself of the hook. For ten strikes the average is one catch.

That particular tarpon was soon at liberty, and in the reaction we were conscious of the closing in of the dusk. The outline of the shore had taken on a sombre tinge, the bay rustled in the evening breeze, and the pelicans which all day flap to and fro along the coast were flying homeward to their rocks. A sense of melancholy

seemed to fall upon Venezuela, settling down for another of her immemorial nights, and in the gathered
gloom the lamps in isolated cottages of Negro fisher-
men were the only signs of life upon the darkness of
that shadowy land.

It was necessary to rise at dawn for the morning fishing, and so, when we had eaten our sandwiches, we
removed our shoes and, dressed as we were, rolled ourselves in the hammocks swung under the rafters of an
open bamboo shed. In that sheltered bay the sea rolled
softly on the beach and its rhythmic beat was like the
stir of another pulse within one's tired brain.

About two o'clock I was awakened by the barking of
dogs and, sitting up, caught the outlines of a man and
woman, accompanied by a mule, slinking by our shelter
on their way to the mountain track beyond. Why they
should have been out at such an hour passes my comprehension; but Venezuelan peons think nothing of travelling night and day from one remote village to another,
and no doubt that couple had some purpose in view.
Their bowed figures were a kind of symbol of Venezuela's history, in which the peasant, dumbly patient
and enduring, has plodded along unchanged, despite
the erratic violence of autocrats and the stony indifference of nature.

I need not say anything more about our fishing. But
I would observe that if those who spend fortunes to
catch tarpon off Florida were to try farther south, the

coast of Venezuela might well become famous among sportsmen. A few miles to the east of La Guaira, at the watering-place of Mercuto, the Government runs an hotel; and if the fishing facilities were properly developed and entrance to Venezuela made easier for visitors —the red tape of forms has surely reached its climax in this country—this hotel might soon return handsome profits, instead of showing, as it did in my day, a large annual deficit.

But there is one inherent drawback. The bathing is dangerous. Sharks and barracuda abound, and though you may scare the sharks by splashing and avoid the barracuda by remaining still, you cannot very well be both noisy and silent at the same instant. Even the fishing is occasionally spoilt by the sharks, who do not hesitate to bite your catch in two if the opportunity occurs. But nothing is altogether perfect in this uncertain world.

We arrived back in Caracas in the afternoon. At my friend's house I was met by the enquiry:

"Are you going to the bullfight? You have just time to get ready."

"No," said I. "I am not going to the bullfight. I intend to have a leisurely shave and a leisurely bath, and then I am going to sleep."

The Background of "Nostromo"

▽

I have already written about Conrad in this book, but the mention, in the last chapter, of La Guiara, the port of South America which he knew best, induces me to add, as a sort of appendix, this essay on "Nostromo." For it was the sight of La Guiara and the atmosphere of Venezuela in general which gave Conrad, in so far as personal experience gave it him, his background for that novel. And if in what follows I go beyond my title, as I assuredly do, may that be overlooked in my desire to do justice to an extraordinary work, which has never, I feel, received sufficient recognition.

CHAPTER XIV

The Background of "Nostromo"

I<small>T IS PERHAPS PERMISSIBLE</small> to begin these remarks by stating that it was my admiration for *Nostromo* which brought about my friendship with Joseph Conrad. In November, 1912, "Rhythm," a long-since defunct review edited by Katherine Mansfield and Mr. Middleton Murry, published an article by me on Conrad which had been written, in the main, to draw attention to the remarkable qualities of *Nostromo*. Mr. Edward Garnett, ever helpful in his encouragement of young writers, sent Conrad a copy of it and he replied, "Would Curle care to see me? That criticism is *something* and no mistake. I am exceedingly pleased. Give him my friendly greeting. . . . I shall ask him down here soon."

And therefore it is with a special feeling that I write once more about *Nostromo*. To me it is not only one of the great novels of the world, but the first link, if I may so phrase it, in a friendship which was to endure to the last moment of Conrad's life. So much for the personal note.

I have recently been rereading *Nostromo* and in doing so emotions aroused by its original perusal, more than twenty-five years ago, have been powerfully recreated. Closing the book, I feel again its magic about me, just as, after listening to a symphony, a transmuted echo of it lingers within the inward ear. For in that novel Conrad conjured up the very atmosphere, material and spiritual, of a whole country, and when one has laid it aside it is as if one were sailing away from Costaguana, which, in the dusk, slowly fades astern.

If it be the genius of a supreme artist to make the places he writes of and the people he describes more vivid than the places and the people we know, then in *Nostromo* Conrad has truly proved himself a supreme artist. For in reading it we actually seem to live in this land of his imagination, we actually seem to meet the people who walk the streets of Sulaco or throng the reception-rooms of the Casa Gould. Indeed, we are caught up in the whirlpool of the Revolution—that Revolution out of whose stress and terror was born the Occidental Republic—and we sense with acute dismay the danger of those friends, who, in their intense vitality, make us, the readers, no more than ghostly companions of their vicissitudes.

And shutting our eyes the scene takes shape before us: the dusty campo with its scattered villages; the range of the cordillera, crowned by the snowy mass of Higuerota; the vast, silent expanse of the Golfo Placido; the pink and white walls of Sulaco; the gorgeous sunsets, blood-red upon the bay, and the cool, pearly dawns cut by the black shadows of the mountains.

And yet, despite its epic spaciousness, *Nostromo* remains the least known of Conrad's greater novels. The principal reason for this is traceable, I suggest, to the complex method of narration, which, in the earlier part of the book, retards the progress of the story and is decidedly bewildering. For example, the escape by sea of the defeated Dictator-President, Don Vincente Ribiera, is briefly described (in the edition I have been reading) on pages 11 to 14, but we then hear nothing more about it till page 224, when his adventures just before his final exit are given in considerable detail in Decoud's letter to his sister. Chronology is discarded in these opening chapters, while the author, as if carried away by his interest in persons and events, follows one lead after another.

Why, we may ask ourselves, did Conrad adopt this indirect approach? The answer, one may suppose, is that he was resolved to build up so convincing an atmosphere that when he did come to picture the events of the Revolution, the country where it was enacted and the people who play their part in it should already have gained our close attention by their profound air of reality. We must read *Nostromo* more as a segment of existence than as an ordinary novel. The characters who move through its pages, with their variety of problem and personality, are yet all influenced by the tragic futility and darkness of the land; and in order to make us feel this blight, so deeply affecting the intermingled lives of every one, Conrad had first to fill in his background to a point where it was almost physically visible.

And to a lesser extent the popularity of *Nostromo* may have suffered from its being a novel neither about the East nor, in essentials, about the sea. This sounds a trivial reason, as, in fact, it is, but man is a creature of habit, and very early in Conrad's career it came to be assumed that when he wrote, his settings must be the Malay Archipelago or the ocean itself. Just as the public rather resents—or, at least, distrusts—a comedian who turns to tragedy or a soldier who becomes a politician, so does it resent, or distrust, an author who strikes out a new line. Even students of Conrad have not, as a rule, taken *Nostromo* as seriously as other of his novels, while I have more than once heard admirers of his work assert that it was the one book of his they had not read. I admit, however, that away back in 1910 Arnold Bennett wrote to me, "I regard *Nostromo* as one of the greatest novels of any age," while somewhere or other Mr. Hilaire Belloc speaks of it as "that extraordinary book." But perhaps he was quoting another's opinion, for my recollection is that, on mentioning his own criticism to him, Mr. Belloc answered that he had no recollection of even having read *Nostromo*. But certainly Bennett had.

Conrad, himself, considered *Nostromo* as "my greatest creative effort." He wrote these very words in a copy of the work, while in his "Author's Note" to the new edition he calls it, "the most anxiously meditated of the longer novels which belong to the period following upon the publication of the *Typhoon* volume of short stories"—it took the better part of the years 1903-4 to write—and he was always particularly pleased when any one displayed an intelligent knowledge of it. The toil of its composition was a terrific strain on him—in mere bulk it is the longest of his books—and though he was philosophic about its failure to win wide popularity, still he felt it keenly. This "dead frost," as he named it to his wife, was dear to his heart and I do not think that he ever really understood why it should have fallen so flat on its first appearance. He informed me that when it was serialized in "T. P.'s Weekly"—what a medium!—readers had inundated the editor with letters of protest, declaring that they had not the vaguest idea what it was all about. But as he received little more than a hundred pounds, one cannot think that the paper did so badly.

There is yet another reason which may conceivably account for the relative unpopularity of *Nostromo*, and that is the title itself. "Nostromo" is a corruption of the Italian words "Nostro Uomo"—"Our Man." It

213

was the name given to Giovanni Fidanza— "Gian Battista" to the Violas—, the "magnificent Capataz de Cargadores," by Captain Mitchell's mispronunciation of the words. And like many another name so given it stuck. But it *has* a rather meaningless sound, not atoned for by anything mysterious or musical, and in my opinion it is not a happy title for a work of such power and originality.

There has been a good deal of discussion as to where precisely in South America Costaguana is supposed to be. But even if it were not stated several times in the book that it is on the West Coast, that fact would be clearly deducible from the description of the country. I have seen places in Peru, where the Andes tower above the plains some sixty miles inland, which could very well stand for Costaguana; and though Conrad had never been in Peru, he had, unquestionably, read sufficient about the West Coast to have grasped the main features of its configuration.

Conrad had, however, as a young sailor aboard a French ship in the 'Seventies, landed in northern South America on a few brief occasions. In some article I wrote I had evidently mentioned that his total stay there did not amount to more than twelve hours, for in 1923 he sent me a letter on the subject. Here is an extract: "As to *No* [*stromo*]. If I ever mentioned 12 hours it must relate to P.[orto] Cabello where I was ashore about that time. In La Guayra [sic] as I went up the hill and had a distant view of Caracas I must have been 2½ to 3 days. It's such a long time ago! And there were a few hours in a few other places on that dreary coast of Ven'la."

It is really amazing to think that Conrad's only physical contact with South America were these scanty days on the coast of Venezuela and that yet, nearly thirty years later, he could evoke its living semblance. But that was how his genius worked. He used to tell me that he had no imagination; and though this, of course, was a mere way of speaking, nevertheless it is true that his imagination was of a type to take fire from an observed fact, however small.

And, after all, La Guaira from the water does seem to epitomize the spirit of Latin America. Under the blazing sun its bright colours, backed by the gloomy mountain, up whose lower slopes climb outlying streets and adobe huts, give it that exotic appearance which speaks of another civilization and produces in one the feeling that here anything might happen. And in the pellucid twilight, when the garish tints of the houses begin to blend beneath the shadow of the hill, then, indeed, the glamour of the tropics rises about one and the romance of a continent, that romance which contains so much that is beautiful and so much that is sordid, unveils itself to one's gaze.

Is it too fanciful to suppose that in the youthful Conrad, pacing in the cool of evening the deck of his ship anchored before La Guaira, the first vague hints of *Nostromo* were already stirring? Who knows? But, in any case, we may assume that when he was actually writing the novel a mental picture of that Venezuelan port must have been constantly before him.

Nostromo himself was suggested by the Dominic of *The Mirror of the Sea*, Antonia Avellanos by his first childish love, and the story of the buried silver Conrad both heard as a yarn and read about in an old volume of reminiscences. We learn these facts from his "Author's Note," while he told a friend of mine that he studied many old prints of South America to stimulate his imagination. But in a sense all this only makes the book the more astonishing. A few casual days ashore in Venezuela, memories of a Mediterranean sailor and a Polish girl, a bookish knowledge of the West Coast littoral, the look of faded prints—these were the poor ingredients which, in the alembic of his genius, produced this great and moving book.

I have mentioned how the spirit of Costaguana affects the characters of *Nostromo*, but there is another spirit, too, which weighs upon many of them—the spirit of the silver mine. It sapped the loyalty of Charles Gould to his wife, it undermined the honour of Nostromo, it awoke the greed of men like Sotillo and Pedro Montero, it cost Decoud his life and Mrs. Gould her happiness. Indeed, the corroding influence of these "material interests" seems in that land of fantastic day-dreams but another emanation of its madness.

The main themes of *Nostromo* may be called the Revolution, the development of the Gould Concession, and the career of Nostromo himself; and all the threads run into one another. But it is the gallery of portraits which remains with us when the details of the story grow dim. And what a gallery it is! Nostromo, successful in everything and yet gnawed by resentment against the very people he serves so well; Charles Gould, with his contempt for fine phrases and his obsession hidden by a silent manner; Mrs. Gould, with her sensitive compassion and her aching heart; Decoud, the scoffer who could not escape his fate; Dr. Monygham, made bitter by atrocious experiences but reborn through his devotion to Mrs. Gould; the old Garibaldino, with his austere thoughts of a loftier age; Captain Mitchell, fussy, simple, self-important and loveable; Don José Avellanos, the patriot with an unflinching soul; Sotillo, the incarnation of avarice, fear and brutality. But why go on? In the multitudinous pages of *Nostromo* people pass and repass, appear and disappear, as in life itself, and in few other novels are there such a crowd of figures and such a universal richness of characterization.

The writing of *Nostromo* is throughout splendidly suited to the epic frame of the story. But if I give here two quotations it is not to prove that point—if, indeed, quotations ever prove such points—, but to show with what imaginative realism Conrad envisaged South America.

Here is dawn in Sulaco during the Revolution:

"Charles Gould turned towards the town. Before him the jagged peaks of the Sierra came out all black in the clear dawn. Here and there a muffled lepero whisked round the corner of a grass-grown street before the ringing hoofs of his horse. Dogs barked behind the walls of the gardens; and with the colourless light the chill of the snows seemed to fall from the mountains upon the disjointed pavements and the shuttered houses with broken cornices and the plaster peeling in patches between the flat pilasters of the fronts. The daybreak struggled with the gloom under the arcades on the Plaza, with no signs of country people disposing their goods for the day's market, piles of fruit, bundles of vegetables ornamented with flowers, on low benches under enormous mat umbrellas; with no cheery early morning bustle of villagers, women, children, and loaded donkeys. Only a few scattered knots of revolutionists stood in the vast space, all looking one way from under their slouched hats for some sign of news from Rincon. The largest of those groups turned round like one man as Charles Gould passed, and shouted, 'Viva la libertad!' after him in a menacing tone."

And here is sunset upon the land:

"The declining sun had shifted the shadows from

218

west to east amongst the houses of the town. It had shifted them upon the whole extent of the immense Campo, with the white walls of its haciendas on the knolls dominating the green distances; with its grass-thatched ranchos crouching in the folds of ground by the banks of streams; with the dark islands of clustered trees on a clear sea of grass, and the precipitous range of the Cordillera, immense and motionless, emerging from the billows of the lower forest like the barren coast of a land of giants. The sunset rays striking the snow-slope of Higuerota from afar gave it an air of rosy youth, while the serrated mass of distant peaks remained black, as if calcined in the fiery radiance. The undulating surface of the forests seemed powdered with pale gold dust; and away there, beyond Rincon, hidden from the town by two wooded spurs, the rocks of the San Tómé gorge, with the flat wall of the mountain itself crowned by gigantic ferns, took on warm tones of brown and yellow, with red rusty streaks, and the dark green clumps of bushes rooted in crevices."

There is the West Coast of South America! There, authentically and for ever! The very breath of it, hot and exciting, comes back to me as I read again these sentences.

I have been visiting various countries in South America off and on for more years than I care to remember and, personally, I should have thought that Conrad's perception of the South American character was striking in its intuitive comprehension. But I believe that both W. H. Hudson and R. B. Cunninghame Graham, writers with a knowledge of that continent infinitely fuller than mine, have questioned his understanding of South American psychology. But even if they are right, what does it matter? If his world is visionary, his people are real—and that is all that ultimately counts. After all, Sir Hugh Clifford, one of the leading authorities on Malaya, has stated that Conrad did not truly understand Malays; and yet Conrad's Malays live.

I have sometimes wondered whether, in some strange way, there is a secret pattern in *Nostromo* of which the author never spoke. In a copy of the book belonging to me Conrad wrote that "it was expanded to this size by the steady contemplation of the possibilities of the subject, and by the ambition to render the spirit of an epoch in the history of Sth. America"; but beneath all that there seems to be something else, something tremendous, which, like a pearl of great price, needs to be diligently searched for. It is, in retrospect, one of my abiding regrets that I did not ask Conrad many more questions about his books; and about none would I have liked to ask more than about *Nostromo*. But Conrad could be very reticent when he chose and perhaps things are better as they are. In the grave stillness which falls upon these pages one feels the solution of a mystery that evades one. The clamour dies, the storm abates, and at long last the petty schemes and sufferings of mankind will be swallowed in a silence as deep as the "solemn hush" that reigns for ever over the Placid Gulf or the "breathless pause" of dusk upon the high sierras.

Four
American Cities

NEW YORK
RICHMOND
CHICAGO
WASHINGTON

▽

A line of steamers runs from La Guaira to New York, by way of Porto Rico—whose capital, San Juan, struck me as being almost entirely devoid of the glamour of the West Indies—, and we may imagine that we have boarded one of those steamers and made the journey, for this chapter begins with a brief description of the largest city in America. It then goes on to describe three other American cities— the four representing, respectively, the North, the South, the Middle West, and the Capital of the Country. They are impressionistic sketches, and their value, if any, lies in that alone.

CHAPTER XV

Four American Cities

New York

Perhaps no great city
can, in its entirety, be viewed at a glance with so complete a success as New York. For no other city has
buildings of such a height and few other cities have, on
the proper day, so crystal-clear an air. May we, therefore, ascend, this fine summer morning, to the summit
of the highest building of all—the Empire State?

The island of Manhattan, outlined by its rivers and
fringed by a multitude of towns and suburbs, lies twelve
hundred feet beneath, one dense, enormous mass of
houses. Yes, just one mass of houses and streets, save
for a few dingy squares and the expanse of Central
Park, which, from this altitude, looks ridiculously
patchy and insignificant. Between its tall dwellings,
the straight, long roadway of Fifth Avenue resembles
a tunnel and the innumerable cars moving up and down
are exactly like so many mechanical toys. And when

they all stop for two minutes out of every five to allow the cross-town traffic to pass one gets the quaint idea that their springs have run down or—in a more poetic mood—that they have been suddenly frozen by a fatal spell.

The great buildings of the city tower far and near like giants amid a swarm of pygmies, and at the foot of the island the skyscrapers about Wall Street, clustered so close together as to seem but different portions of one fabulous palace, front the waters of the bay to form a magnificent gateway to a continent. Out there, on its tiny islet, the Statue of Liberty appears no larger than a thimble, while the tugs, puffing up and down the Hudson and the East River, resemble those fussy aquatic beetles which must be always on the move, skating hither and thither without apparent purpose.

On the water itself strange shadows come and go and the ripple of the boats writes feathery designs upon the rivers' calm. The funnels of Atlantic liners tied up to the docks are scarcely larger than ordinary chimneys and the trains on the Elevated Railroad seem to crawl from station to station. As to individual people, they are but specks of irrelevant dust or, if you choose, earth-bound insects emerging from, or diving into, their holes.

The entire island, indeed, looks absurdly small and cramped, and it is only when the eye wanders beyond it to the vast, flat sections of Brooklyn, Queens and the

Bronx and to the row of New Jersey towns which hang upon the farther shore of the Hudson that one can really believe that here, within the radius of one's vision, some ten million people are living.

An ocean haze rests upon the bay and in the middle distance the form of Staten Island is vague. But where the inlets of the sea pierce the marshes of New Jersey, the water gleams beneath the sun and the whole of that desolate region takes on rare and singular patterns. The huge George Washington Bridge across the Hudson, which, seen near by, is one of the wonders of the world, is quite unimposing from this pinnacle, and as for the five bridges that span the East River, why, one feels that one could just pick them up one after the other.

A deep sound, the sound of the great city, floats up everlastingly. There is something mournful about it, as though, in its dull monotony, it were the emanation of countless human sighs. And, in truth, from up here this enormous town *has* the appearance of a prison from which there could be no escape. It spreads in all directions, soiled by the dust of years and with an air of mean uniformity, save where the watch-towers of jailers—the skyscrapers—break the lines; and once within its coils it is as if a victim must be lost for ever.

And yet how noble is the total effect as one walks around the parapet, how ample and varied the panorama which unfolds itself. There is something exhilarating in sheer size and in the contemplation of man's mightiest labours, and gazing down upon this city size and labour seem to have reached their ultimate climax, if not to the actual, at least to the mind's, eye. And in these shimmering, changing scenes of land and water, in this stupendous map which includes sea and city and distant range, both grandeur and beauty are to be found.

Richmond

The Americans, who at heart have a strong sentiment for tradition, have a special feeling for Virginia, and its Southern spirit is fostered as much by the North as by the South. The Settlement of the Seventeenth Century, the Rebellion of the Eighteenth, the Civil War of the Nineteenth were so largely bound up with Virginian soil that the Old Dominion is richer in romantic associations than is any other State. And Richmond, as its capital, seems to concentrate within itself the history, the glamour, the very spirit of Virginia.

Defeat has given to the past an emotional, tragic vividness, and in this town of statues and monuments, of houses inhabited long since by famous men, every step recalls historic names and stirring scenes. Indeed, one has only to walk through Richmond to feel around one the breath of other days, so passionately does she guard her Southern ideals and memories.

It is true that there has sprung up about old Richmond a modern, industrial city of some two hundred thousand inhabitants, but that has not really changed its inner tone. If anything, it has thrown it into higher relief and caused the vanished age to impress itself more vividly.

Sitting in the gardens of the Capitol, that stately building designed by Jefferson, where Lafayette was entertained, where Chief Justice Marshall presided at the trial for treason of Aaron Burr, where President Davis thundered his defiance of the North, where General Lee received command of the armies of the State, one might fondly persuade oneself that time had been rolled back.

And especially is this so on a spring day when, in the renewed green of the earth, everything seems young again. In the soft quiet of such an afternoon it would be easy to dream oneself into any epoch, and it requires no rare flight of fancy to imagine that those people now sitting on the benches are the same as those who must have been sitting on them seventy-six years ago, discussing the ominous storm-mutterings that were swelling louder with each hour.

This section of the town has altered relatively little, and one's musings are not interrupted by any gross incongruity. Richmond, indeed, must have looked very like this on that April day of 1861 when the State Convention voted to secede. Very like it: the old South's spacious charm still rests upon these gardens.

But perhaps the best way of all to catch the flavour

229

of the Richmond that was is to stroll up in the evening
to the high ground of Monument Avenue. There, in
the dignity of bronze, stand, apart from one another in
their green plots, three Southern figures of renown—
Robert E. Lee, Joseph E. Johnston, Jefferson Davis.

Lee, the greatest of them all, looks superb on his
horse. As darkness advances his statue glimmers more
and more sombrely against the sky and, as it melts
slowly, irresistibly, into the gloom, seems to symbolize
in itself the chivalrous ardour and utter failure of the
Southern cause. Knightly and defiant to the last, it
evanesces before a force too mighty to be controlled.

.   .   .   .   .

Motoring out of Richmond along the James River I
came, some twenty miles away, upon a large farm—
now, if I remember, used for training race horses
—called "Curle's Neck." As my name is an unusual
one, I was interested in this and asked Mr. James
Branch Cabell, who, besides being a writer of distinction, is an authority on Virginia genealogy, how it was
derived. He answered that it was simply the old spell-
ing of "curl" and that the farm was called after a curl
or twist in the river's neck.

I gave the matter no further thought, but a few years
later, when I was staying with friends who had the most
lovely old house and park about fifty miles above Richmond, I was shown a printed family history and in it,

to my astonishment, I saw the name of a Curle—he had a wife and five children—who had intermarried with the family in the Eighteenth Century. And none of us knew it when the invitation was given! So perhaps Mr. Cabell was wrong and my Virginia "cousins" are really my cousins. I certainly hope so and, in any case, it is an excellent excuse for dedicating my book to such hospitable and charming people.

Presumably the Curle mentioned above is the one who put this somewhat dubious advertisement into the "Virginia Gazette" of January 12, 1769:

"There will be exposed for sale for ready cash at Petersburg, the 16th. of this instant (January) a parcel of Negroes.

WILLIAM R. CURLE, Adm."

Nice friendly word, "parcel!"

I trust that this interruption is not totally out of place. The coincidence—maybe, even, a double coincidence—seems too pat not to mention.

Chicago

Chicago leaves on one a sense of chaotic, sprawling vastness, and in winter the icy winds off Lake Michigan have a wild vitality fitting to the spirit of the town. It is, indeed, a city of extremes—extreme cold and extreme heat, extreme grandeur and extreme squalor. It has a splendid frontage along the shore, but if you look backwards from the top of one of its buildings, it is as if you were looking upon a city of tenements.

The pulse of rushing life is even more pronounced in Chicago than it is in New York, and the Loop, on which everything seems to converge, is its beating heart. There, truly, one feels the mighty urge, the eager youth, of the great city and becomes conscious of that something monstrous and yet naïve which is Chicago's personality. High endeavour and deep evil flourish side by side, and Chicago, for all its amenities and sophistication, has a touch of the prairie about it—it has been commented on before—, a touch, one might say, of the hobldehoy.

I was taken, of course, to see the stockyards and my friend was surprised, and even pained, when I flatly refused to watch animals being slaughtered. It was quite bad enough to watch them being got ready for slaughter or lying in slaughtered heaps about the floor. I cannot rid my mind of the remembrance of a huge hall, on to which I looked down from a bridge that spanned it, which was full of dead and dying animals, gore, and blood-stained butchers. Into this hall railway trucks, packed with cattle, were being shunted; and the bellowing, terrified brutes were driven from them into the arena by men armed with long poles at the end of which there was an electric prod. It was all too sickening. As for the pigs, in batches they were herded from pen to pen, each higher than the last, until they reached the topmost one of all, where a cord was attached to their hind legs and they were whirled upwards, around a huge wheel and along a pulley only to have their squeals quenched in a kind of gurgling sigh. We were made to follow through the building the dead pigs, which perform that journey on a moving platform and get whiter and more disjointed at every step. I am far from a vegetarian, but I might become one soon if I were to witness again what I witnessed on that day.

We lunched with the managerial staff of one of the Stockyard companies. It was a Saturday, I believe, and the yards would cease work early. It was then getting on for midday and seeing large numbers of animals still alive in the outer pens, I asked one of my hosts whether they would be kept there till Monday.

"Oh, no," he answered casually, "they'll all be worked off by two!"

It struck me as being an utterly heartless remark by a man who was probably an excellent citizen and a kind father. But Chicago has no use for sentiment of that sort. Even human beings have to look after themselves or go under. It is the cruel, simple philosophy of the Frontier.

The thirty-mile drive to Lake Forest is very fine and the mansions of the wealthy, which line it, are surrounded by sumptuous gardens. And yet on that drive, where one breathed an atmosphere of millionaires, there was a typical thing which awoke in me again that sense of paradox and extremes on which Chicago seems to flourish. One short section of that perfect road was as rough as an old-fashioned country lane: apparently it was a no-man's land between two townships and nobody would do anything about it.

I spent only a few days in Chicago, but they were during the "boom" period when its roaring, rampant tide was at the full, and I shall never forget its effect on me. It was a stimulating effect, but it was also rather unnerving. To ride the whirlwind—and one need not encounter gunmen to have that feeling—is not to be soothed.

Washington

Mid-November is doubtless not the best time to visit Washington, for what city looks its handsomest when the leaves are falling and the air is touched with winter? But on the other hand perhaps one gathers at this season a juster idea of the city itself than one would in summer, when it is embowered in greenery and its contours are blurred. Now, so to say, its skeleton stands clearly forth; and as official Washington is constructed mainly of white granite and white marble, which, seen from above, bear some resemblance to ribs of bone, the word is not so very far-fetched.

Study it, then, with me from the top of the Washington Monument, that monolith which towers to a height

234

of five hundred and fifty-five feet. North, east and west it spreads before one, covering, with its park areas, the sixty-nine square miles of the District of Columbia and overflowing into the State of Maryland; while to the south the Potomac winds to the sea, with the wooded hills of Virginia beyond. It is a view which calls up, in its historic landmarks, the very spirit of the Republic. There to the north lies the White House, backed by the Presidential gardens; there to the east, the Capitol, whose dome is so enormous as to dwarf even a building eight and a half acres in extent; due west, at the end of the long and narrow Reflecting Pool, which mirrors, it, as it mirrors the Washington Monument, rises, in solitary beauty, the Greek Temple which is the Lincoln Memorial; while southward, across the river, white amid the autumn trees, the pillars of Arlington show up distinctly.

And with this bird's-eye view one perceives what, from below, appeared puzzling about the lay-out of the city. While the streets run parallel with one another and cross at right-angles, as in so many American towns, Washington has also numerous avenues that bisect the streets diagonally and meet at circles dotted here and there throughout the city. Thus a map of Washington gives an illusion as of wheels, large and small, superimposed upon the regularity of the streets. The city was thus designed, I gather, to facilitate a massing of troops at strategic points in case of invasion. Which sounds, does it not, like the good old days of redcoats and stone forts?

The architects of modern, as of old, Washington have achieved a remarkable distinction, a distinction which throws into painful prominence those Nineteenth Century atrocities which in Washington, as in London, speak of the degradation of a great art. What we, in England, call the "Victorian Era" in architecture, the Americans call the "General Grant Period," and, as with us, that may include anything from sham Gothic to a dreadful bare ugliness. But Washington, under the influence of a long-sighted and harmonious building plan, is rapidly obliterating the stigma. A restrained stateliness of outline is now the note, and nothing could be more appropriate.

Some of the smaller edifices, such as those of the Pan-American Union, with its Spanish patio, the Folger Library, which houses in matchless style the finest of all Shakespearean collections, and the Freer Art Gallery, with its Oriental paintings and porcelains, are among the choicest. But then, again, there is a special appeal about those Washington buildings of immense size in which the proportions are perfectly balanced and blended. Consider, in this light, the Department of Commerce, which is one thousand and fifty feet long, or the hall of the Union Station, which is seven hundred and fifty feet long. They have a magnificence of their own and seem

236

somehow to suggest a parable of America's teeming greatness.

Straight down Pennsylvania Avenue from the Capitol, at a distance of about a couple of miles, stands the White House, a building which in national significance is second to none throughout the land. In appearance it resembles a Georgian country mansion of moderate size, with two long, low basement wings. Most of the lawns and gardens lie at the back, but those in front are open to strollers and people are always walking nonchalantly about them.

The State Apartments are a suite of five rooms on the ground floor: the Dining Room, panelled in wood and capable of seating about a hundred guests; the Green Room, the Blue Room, the Red Room, elegant salons opening one into the other and named for the colour schemes of their decoration; and, finally, the East Room, which runs through the house and is eighty-two feet long by forty wide.

A rather grand simplicity, combining well the Republican idea with the dignity of the Presidential office, is the keynote of the White House. And think of the illustrious men who have lived within its walls and helped to mould here the policy of the United States! One might well fancy that when the quietness of night settles upon these rooms ghostly forms emerge and people them. For history has left its mark upon this house and it carries a weight of memories.

237

There are no sentries outside the White House, though the grounds are patrolled by guards in ordinary clothes. And that, again, is typical of the inner simplicity which rules its life. Everything is unostentatious, but everything is in good taste. Even the Negro footmen—"ushers" is, I believe, the correct American term—in their blue tails, striped waistcoats and silver buttons, have an air of friendliness which would be utterly impossible in an English footman. But then England and America are so profoundly unalike in their general approach that the fact of their having a common language sometimes strikes a visitor as an astonishing coincidence.

Over fifty statues of political and military personalities adorn the squares and circles of Washington. This, in itself, would suggest that one was in the capital of a large country; but when, added to that, one notices so very many big hotels and elaborate churches, it is almost unnecessary to enquire further. A floating population and a diverse piety of such dimensions are only associated, as a rule, with a centre of government.

And yet, with it all, there is a hint of something provincial about Washington, as if its international outlook could not altogether conceal the underlying Main Street. And I suppose that that is only natural; after all, its population reflects inevitably the population of ten thousand Main Streets throughout the land.

238

Reflections at Newton's Birthplace

▽

There would seem to be no association between this chapter and the last; but, as will presently be made apparent, Sir Isaac Newton's name is connected in my mind with the name of another great physicist now living in America and eventually to become an American citizen. Moreover, there are numerous references to representative Americans in the pages that follow; and so, taking one thing with another, I feel able to place this chapter here without any deep feeling of discord.

CHAPTER XVI

Reflections at Newton's Birthplace

W<small>HEN I WAS MOTORING</small> with friends through Lincolnshire in the summer of 1935 we stopped off at Woolsthorpe to see the house where Sir Isaac Newton was born. It is a little old manor house, now a farm, and over the door, carved in the stone perhaps a hundred and fifty years ago, is the bare statement that he was born there. The farmer's wife obligingly allowed us to enter and showed us the actual room. We asked her whether there was a visitors'-book and she answered, yes, there was a book in which people sometimes wrote their names, and produced it for us. It was a dilapidated object, fast falling to pieces, but as we idly turned the pages, we came, about three years back, on the name of Albert Einstein.

This interested me greatly, not only because it seemed so fitting, but because it appeared to show that the aloof Professor felt that desire, which is felt by millions of ordinary people, to see the birthplaces and the graves of famous persons. I often think that this desire has a double foundation: one likes to have the past recalled by such tangible evidences and one likes to be able to say that one *has* seen such places. A harmless, prevalent form of vanity to which I now intend to give way, not, however, without an underlying humility when I consider how many such places I have not seen and never now will see.

The most impressive grave in the world is, I suppose, that of Cecil Rhodes in the Matopo hills in Rhodesia. Rhodes, himself, chose the site because of its solitary grandeur; and, indeed, that view over a sea of rugged, desolate hills, that wide view in which the spirit of savage Africa seems to brood in the dark mystery of her heart, is one of the most majestic imaginable. I have often climbed those rocks and stood by Rhodes's grave, gazing over the wilderness, as he had gazed.

I can, in a way, understand why he should have wanted to be buried there, and yet it has always seemed rather queer to me that people should mind where they are buried—personally, I even find it rather hard to understand why anybody should want to be buried and not cremated—; but if there is sentiment about it, then Buckle, the historian of civilization, should, beyond question, be sleeping peacefully amid the apricot groves outside Damascus. The surroundings are truly beautiful and I used to stand by that railed-off plot and dream in the dappled quiet of the afternoon.

Another beautiful setting for a grave is Dryburgh Abbey, where, within sound of the Tweed and with the noble old ruins as protection, lies Sir Walter Scott, with Field-Marshal Lord Haig beside him. My grandfather knew Sir Walter well, and at the funeral of Tom Purdy, his faithful henchman, the novelist addressed a few remarks to my father's eldest brother, who was then a small boy. This uncle of mine died some forty years ago, but I recall him perfectly. Thus I have spoken to a man who had spoken to Sir Walter Scott. And to whom had Sir Walter not spoken?—George IV, Byron, almost every contemporary of note. It is a curious reflection.

Talking of Scottish writers, though I have visited neither the birth- nor the burial-place of Robert Burns, yet I have seen a room in which he once spent a night. At one period of his chequered life he rented a farm from my Dumfriesshire cousins and on a certain occasion, being storm-bound when at their house, he slept in their kitchen. And that, too, is curious to reflect on.

I suppose that the two most famous graves in the world are those of Shakespeare at Stratford-on-Avon and of Washington at Mount Vernon. I have been to both of them, but they are *so* famous that to see them at last was almost like an anticlimax. It would be practically impossible for them to come up to expectation, and I am inclined to think that the graves of lesser known celebrities can move one more. What, for instance,

243

could give one a stranger sensation than to see Pizarro lying in his glass coffin in the cathedral at Lima in Peru—I cannot actually remember, by the way, whether I ever did see it, though I seem to recall its precise location: it is all so long since—or to stand by the flagstone of Jane Austen's grave in Salisbury Cathedral? In that cathedral I was also shown six great urns, in one of which, though which one nobody knows, are the remains of Canute. Jane Austen and Canute under the same roof until the Day of Judgement!

Why is it that the tombs of famous generals have almost invariably a heavy, gloomy, funereal aspect? Is it meant to suggest something martial or is it mere chance? I cannot answer the question, but I do know that Napoleon's tomb in the Invalides, Wellington's tomb in St. Paul's, and Grant's tomb on Riverside Drive have that something in common which, to me, is decidedly dismal. Better the plain slabs of Westminster Abbey, with their brief inscriptions, which cover so many famous statesmen and writers, which cover the Unknown Warrior, himself, than all the pomp of St. Paul's Cathedral.

Cathedrals, of course, are the mausoleums of the world, but I think that the cathedral grave which has most appealed to me is that of the Black Prince in Canterbury, with his actual armour and gauntlets hung above it: it is somehow touching in its intimacy. On the confines of that town, I may add, is a grave I can never visit without emotion—the grave of Joseph Conrad. I remember too well the day on which I saw his coffin lowered into it.

I cannot forgive myself for not going, when in Rome, to visit the graves of Keats and Shelley—both dying so young, so full of genius, in a foreign land they must stir one's feelings—, but I have, naturally, seen the graves of Tennyson and Browning in Westminster Abbey. But official graves like those appear to me to be lacking in sentiment and if I were a celebrity, and cared a jot about such things, I would insist on being buried in a country churchyard—not in a country church, I emphasize, as Lord Beaconsfield is, all too gaudily, at Hughenden—but in the churchyard itself. Some really have so restful an air that one might almost be lulled into the belief that death was but a physical trance. Oddly enough, one of the most charming of all, with a weathered, age-old peacefulness, is in Barbados. It was the one spot on that rather dreary island which attracted me.

While there is an interest in looking at the graves of illustrious persons, especially when one comes upon them unexpectedly, yet, after all, they speak of death, and it is more profitable to see where they lived and worked. Gad's Hill has to some visitors, though not, I confess, to me, an atmosphere of Dickens about it still; Bunyan's home in Bedfordshire is just as bare and humble as one would have expected; Poe's cottage in

Fordham has the queer individuality of his tales; and the house in Gardiner, Maine, used by Benedict Arnold just before his Expedition to Canada in 1775 has its Colonial atmosphere unchanged. And if one may carry the matter a step farther, I would add that the Tower of London calls up no more vividly the stilted romances of Harrison Ainsworth than does the House of Seven Gables in Salem, Massachusetts, create the eerie feeling of Hawthorne's famous romance.

The capital idea of the London County Council in placing plaques on the houses inhabited at one time or another by people of note has been copied to some extent in New York, and in both cities one is constantly being surprised on one's strolls. All the same, there is a certain uniformity about town houses which tends to stultify the imagination and I have derived more pleasure from seeing Victor Hugo's house in Guernsey or Walt Whitman's birthplace at Huntington, Long Island, than in seeing where Johnson or Thackeray lived in London. (I had better admit here that I have come upon so many houses in London with plaques on them that I really cannot say whether I have seen these particular ones or not. It goes to prove my point, I think.)

I have made but few conscious pilgrimages in the track of the renowned, but there are some places I *would* like to see, places which seem peculiarly bound up with the people who dwelt there. I would like to

246

see Haworth where the Brontes lived, I would like to see Yasnaya Polyana where Tolstoy lived, I would like to see Goethe's house in Weimar, I would like to see the summer-house, if it be still standing, where Flaubert toiled over his novels. And I would like to have seen Sir Thomas Browne's house in Norwich, which must, I fancy, have been very typical of him; but on enquiring for it in that town, I was told that it no longer existed. When was it pulled down, I wonder? Another house completely bound up with its owner is Abbotsford, which was not only the home but the creation of Sir Walter Scott. That house I know well and it has the indubitable stamp of Sir Walter, who, about the past, was both romantic and inaccurate, on its every stone.

To turn into museums the houses of great men is an idea which appeals to me. It is done more often, perhaps, in America than in England, and, apart from George Washington's home, I have visited the delightful homes of Thomas Jefferson in Virginia and of Andrew Jackson in Tennessee. But there is a danger that such houses, through the generosity of devotees, get overfurnished and the personality of the former owners be lost in the museum atmosphere. However, that is a minor point.

Almost anything to do with certain people is of interest, but they must be people who were remarkable, not alone for their gifts, but for their personalities. To see the house in Washington into which the dying Lincoln was carried—I have also seen the Kentucky log-cabin where he was born—, to see the island of Nevis where Nelson made his disastrous marriage, to see Ephesus, all-ruined in the Anatolian waste, where Paul thundered, gave me a sense of tragic romance; but I have no particular wish to see places connected with the lives of many other persons just as famous. It is not that their achievements leave me cold—I am fairly eclectic—, it is simply that they do not interest me as human beings.

I trust that these reflections, which deal so frequently with the end of man's life, are not of too depressing a nature. But if they are, it is not I who ought to be blamed. Certainly not. The people who ought to be blamed are Sir Isaac Newton and Professor Einstein.

.   .   .   .   .

I wrote this chapter in New York one May morning and later in the day, when a friend came to call, I read it aloud to her.

"Do you know that this is Memorial Day," she said when I had finished, "the national holiday on which America celebrates her fallen soldiers?"

I had not given it a thought, but, taken all in all, it seems so appropriate that on this particular day I should have been writing this particular chapter I venture to mention it here.

248

Bermuda Between Seasons

▽

I saw no birthplaces or graves of famous people in Bermuda and do not even know whether there are any to see; and that is one of the reasons why this chapter comes where it does. After all, there is a certain relief in meeting only one's own kind, even in memory, and in being put to no intellectual strain. Indeed, there is a certain relief in being, at times, entirely by oneself. But even had I been unable to find the faintest reason for writing about this island—and the reason I have given is as faint as it could well be —I would have written about it anyhow. For it is a delectable spot and one well worth recalling to memory.

CHAPTER XVII

Bermuda Between Seasons

THE LAST TWO WEEKS OF May are probably the quietest time of the year in Bermuda, the quietest and the most lovely. The large hotels have closed—at least, they had when I was there some years back—the visitors have tailed off, and Bermuda rests for a brief spell between her winter and her summer seasons. She rests as a great flowery garden rests on a drowsy afternoon, enticing to the sight and full of languorous repose.

And, truly, the island in the month of May is one bountiful garden. The hedgerows blaze with hibiscus and oleander and convolvulus, flowers bloom plentifully, and the junipers (usually called cedars), which crown every rise, give to the whole scene a touch of shady coolness beneath the torrid sun. Blue birds and cardinals fly from tree to tree and, in the brilliance of their plumage, typify the spirit of the Bermudian spring.

But I suppose that the ultimate charm of the island is

in her shallow seas. Like all waters lying within the confines of coral reefs they are of marvellous purity. Bright blues and greens merge into one another, waxing and waning with the cloud effects as though some vast kaleidoscope were revolving beneath the surface. The sea is alive with glitter, with leaping dazzle, and seems to be laughing to itself in young gladness. To sit on some balcony overlooking Hamilton harbour and gaze out across the Great Sound is to start the day as it ought to be started in Bermuda. In the distance stretches the curved horn of the island, culminating in the Admiralty dockyard, and between lies the bay, sown with wooded islets, one beyond the other. They look as if they were poised delicately on the water, ready to take flight together, like a flock of giant sea birds, at the slightest invasion of their retreat. It is a glowing, rippling sight, a sight not easily to be matched.

Talk of the sea suggests bathing, and I presume that Elbow Beach, with its broad sands, is the most popular bathing place in Bermuda. But it did not appeal to me. When I go swimming I prefer an æsthetic to a gregarious pleasure—though the latter is not to be despised—and in Bermuda I know of secluded little bays, sheltered by high banks and calm as inland lakes, where one could float on one's back in a profound peace of sky and water. Few things can be more delicious: in utter solitude one seems, in the faint rise and fall, to be moving effortlessly through space, as though released for ever from all earth entanglements. And then to recline upon the empty sands, to smoke a cigarette, while the warm sun plays about one's limbs and fills one, in the morning light, with a sense of perfect well-being!

Bermuda, which derives seventy-five per cent of her revenue from visitors, has naturally developed her attractions to the best of her ability. But it is a pity that she should try to tickle the palate by a kind of conventional romance. There is quite enough real romance on the island without attempting to gild it. For example, there are subterranean caves in Bermuda, caves going straight down into the rock, fantastic in stalagmite and stalactite, with hushed, dim pools in their recesses; but the glamour of them, the feeling of awe which they evoke, is rather cheapened by giving them such names as "Crystal" and "Wonderland," while their mysterious appeal half-vanishes when one learns that they are lit by electricity. Romance, like poetry, should leave something unsaid, and such caves ought to be explored by lamplight alone. I am glad to think that there must be other undiscovered, nameless caves in Bermuda, dark, dangerous caves, "sleeping untroubled since the beginning of ages."

There are certain obvious attractions which need organization—golf, dancing, bathing, if you choose; but surely nature's attractions might be left to take care of themselves. That, maybe, is a counsel of perfection, and, of course, one must admit that some forms of exploitation are justifiable. For instance, it is pleasant to be sailed out to the reefs and to be shown that bizarre, prismatic world through a glass-bottomed boat—pleasant even if artificial. But why, by all that is fitting, call them "sea gardens"? That pseudo-romantic phraseology is infinitely less suggestive than the real name. "Coral reefs" conjures up all sorts of visions, but "sea gardens" is mere prettiness. However, I take it people know their own business.

Considering the long history of Bermuda and the part she has played for centuries in events of importance, the island, it struck me, was curiously lacking in the atmosphere of an historic background. Even in the dusk I was not conscious of that burdened feeling which imperceptibly pervades those places where men have hoped and suffered. Perhaps the apparent absence of old buildings is the cause of this or perhaps it is simply due to the feeling of lightness in the air. But whatever the explanation, it was as I have said. Bermuda, for all one senses, might be one of those happy isles that have no history, instead of being, in more interpretations than one, the "vexed Bermoothes" of over three hundred years.

The continuity of Bermuda's history gives it, indeed, a special claim to attention, and there is real romance in the thought that her House of Assembly has been in existence since 1620. This venerable body of thirty-six members still functions as vigorously as ever; and to attend a sitting of it, as I did, was to feel the bridging of the years and to perceive that Bermuda has a life of her own which has nothing to do with hotels or visitors. That is to say, nothing to do inherently, although it is plain that an island of thirty thousand inhabitants, which caters for many more than that number of guests every year, cannot ignore the strangers within her gates. And she does not try to ignore them; on the contrary, she lays herself out to welcome them. But if the Bermudian draws one kind of sustenance from America, he draws another kind from his own island, and there is no one with a robuster patriotism.

And not only for Bermuda, but for England. The House of Assembly is modelled in all essential details on the House of Commons and there is even a mace brought in by a Sergeant-at-Arms and laid crosswise on a table beneath the Speaker. The attitude of the legislators is one of Bermuda for the Bermudians, and the Bermudians for the Empire. This loyalty is what one finds all through the small, far islands of the British Empire and is based, seemingly, on an emotion that is almost mystical. A majority of these islanders have never been to England; but many regard it, sentimentally, as "home."

Not having been in Bermuda since Prohibition was repealed in the United States, I am unable to say whether society—I refer to the society of hotels—still leads that hectic and drifting life it used to lead when Bermuda was a "wet" oasis, a paradise of escape. Even in May, when the tempo was so reduced, a good many visitors, from my observation, felt somewhat vague as to where they actually were and knew the Hamilton bars much better than the island beaches. Well, well, if they were enjoying themselves, what of it? And after all, they are rather attractive bars, with gardens attached, and an air of "stay all day and have a jolly time" about them. The worst of it is that the jolliness is so transitory and the aftermath so unpleasant. But that is something people must work out for themselves. The world is altogether too full of dogmatic moralists and nothing is more fatuous than trying to force upon others your own ideas of happiness.

I missed a great book "find" in Hamilton, simply, I fear, because I was not keeping my eyes as wide open as I usually do. For it is my habit, when visiting a new town, to browse over its second-hand bookshops. Such places are fascinating in themselves, and one never knows what lurking treasures may emerge. But I was thinking of spring when I was in Bermuda, not of books, and I let my opportunity slip. A friend of mine, who went there shortly after I returned to America, bought in a Hamilton bookshop for threepence a copy of one of the four anonymous volumes which Galsworthy, before he became famous, wrote under the pseudonym, "John Sinjohn." Back in New York he sold it, at my

256

urgent advice, for twelve hundred and fifty dollars. Not bad! And presumably all the time it was there, under my very nose, while I was airily walking the streets. Too bad! And yet I have had luck of that sort in my time. Once on the Parade in Cape Town I acquired for sixpence another of these anonymous Galsworthys. Only there were no twelve hundred and fifty dollar prices for first editions of Galsworthy in those days! No, and there never will be again.

In their very essence hotels are international and visitors carry into them their own alien atmosphere. And that is why one must get away from Hamilton, the centre of hotel life, if one wants to learn anything about Bermuda. I have nothing against Hamilton, which is a bright and prosperous little town, except that it is not Bermuda. This island has a personality which, like some shy and radiant butterfly, is difficult to catch if pursued, but which may suddenly be glimpsed tantalizingly near by when least expected. It is in her inland groves or by the shores of her solitary bays that it steals upon one, especially, it always seemed to me, on late afternoons, before the twilight has fallen but when the heat of the day has gone. To stroll about Bermuda at such an hour is to discover the island. It is not a discovery that will come, in its fullness, all at once, for nothing so subtle as personality is truly revealed at a glance, but gradually and charmingly, as if a veil were being slowly lifted. You may find it in St. George's at one end, or, more probably, in Somerset at the other.

This last, in its fertile exuberance and the special glory of its hedges, in its freedom from tourists and the variety of its scenery, was for me the very core of Bermuda. I could imagine passing months there in a sort of timeless quiet, and imagine it the more readily because the rents of bungalows in Somerset are, or were, surprisingly low. It was Mr. Hervey Allen, then distinguished as a poet and as the biographer of Poe and later to be world-famous as a novelist, who gave me that information. He and his wife were living in a Somerset bungalow and the afternoon I spent with them is one of my happiest recollections of Bermuda.

It surprised me to hear what he said, for one does not usually associate cheapness with Bermuda, where groaning about hotel prices is not merely a commonplace but a bond of union, but in 1928, at any rate, one *could* live cheaply in Somerset; and well, too, if not exactly like a lord. I am astonished that the honeymoon couples, to whom the island makes such a perennial appeal, have not found that out long ago.

Yes, Bermuda is full of wedded lovers, good luck to them, but I used to take my after-dinner walks alone. The air was cool and fragrant and the lights across the bay gave a touch of comfort to the enfolding dark. The croaking of innumerable frogs, a sound which always suggests to me the joy of nature in mere existence, enhanced one's own sense of life, and the whole island seemed to pulse with the stir of spring. It was not the night of the tropics, which is sometimes almost too overwhelming, nor was it the night of northern climes; it was Bermuda's own night, the night of this flowery island lying snugly in the middle seas.

Strange Happenings

THE SNAKE
THE UNKNOWN
THE MONSTER
THE LIMIT

▽

A decidedly strange thing happened to me in Bermuda, but it was not one of those things which calls for relation. One might say, indeed, that life is full of strange happenings which do not call for relation and that the most exciting events of one's existence are seldom discussed. But the thought of that adventure in Bermuda has suggested some other rather odd adventures which, it appears to me, may be worth recording. They were, I am conscious, nothing much in themselves, but they are easy to talk about and they left their impression.

CHAPTER XVIII

Strange   Happenings

The Snake

Cobras, due doubtless to the food problem, show a liking for the vicinity of mankind which is entirely one-sided and have a disconcerting trick of appearing close to houses from nowhere in particular.   All they want is to be allowed near the chickens; all they do is to frighten people into fits.

I remember that when I was staying with friends in a rather wild part of the Transvaal, I had several encounters with cobras.   The first was simple enough.   I was walking along a path over a rough field and had a gun in my hand because I was shooting rabbits.   Naturally I was on the elert, which was perhaps just as well, as all at once I perceived about thirty yards ahead of me a vicious little head appear suddenly round the corner of an ant-heap and then as suddenly disappear. The course of the path led, I judged, within a foot of the ant-heap and I got the very unpleasant impression that that snake was lying in wait for me and would strike as I passed. No doubt I was mistaken, for cobras, I take it, do not calculate like human beings, but it really gave one an eerie feeling.

I waited until the head appeared again and then I blew it off. Afterwards I measured the snake. It was four and a half feet long, a big cobra of the ordinary brown variety.

My second experience was more exciting and, in a grim way, more amusing. It occurred a few days later.

On this occasion I was merely going for a walk and had nothing with me but a stick. I was forcing my way through a thicket close to the house when I saw, coiled up on a bed of leaves under a tree, an immense black cobra. Now, I do not imagine that black cobras are more venomous than brown ones; but they look more venomous. I debated whether to take a chance with my stick, but decided that unless I managed to break its back with the first blow, the chances would be all with the cobra. So I returned immediately to the house and reported its presence to my host.

"Why didn't you kill it?" he asked with a surprised air.

I explained as well as I could that it might have killed me, but he was not impressed.

"You might have tried," he grumbled.

I could not agree with him: it suggested too obviously

a parody on Tennyson's line, " 'Tis better to have loved and lost than never to have loved at all."

I could see that he still thought poorly of my action, but we got our guns and went to the spot. The cobra had disappeared.

"We'll have to put out bait for it," announced my friend, as if I had given him a good deal of unnecessary trouble.

A length of drainage-pipe was procured and carried to where I had seen the snake. One end was stuffed tight with straw, the other end was left open. Inside the pipe food was placed.

The next day, sure enough, a native "boy," who had been told off for the job, reported that the cobra was in the pipe and, having eaten heartily, was now asleep.

"Stuff up the other end and bring the pipe here," was the order.

"Here" was a bare patch of lawn just outside the house.

The pipe was duly stuffed—not by me—and brought along. My host, who had gone inside, emerged with his gun.

"Now this is what you do," he explained. "You tilt up the pipe and then you begin to pull the straw from the bottom. Then, when the snake comes out, I'll shoot it. Do you follow?"

I followed clearly enough, but I felt no enthusiasm for the job.

"Come on now, get started!"

He stood well behind the pipe, while the "boy" and I raised it to the correct angle and then, with our free hands, began very gingerly to remove the straw. That is to say, we were extremely slow in putting our hands up the pipe and extremely fast in drawing them away.

Before long it became only too apparent that the wall of straw was growing thin and that the cobra (by now, indubitably, in a vile temper) was likely to bolt at any instant. The native "boy" sensibly concluded that he had done his share of the work, and though he continued to support the pipe, he discontinued his efforts in the other direction. I longed to follow his example.

"Hurry up! Hurry up!"

My host was right to be impatient: one man had stopped work, the other was showing visible reluctance.

With infinite caution I put my hand up the pipe once more; and it seems to me, in recollection, that its swift withdrawal was about six inches ahead of the snake. I expect I exaggerate, but I can assure you that an angry cobra moves quick as lightning.

It emerged like a black streak and slithered away over the ground. But before it could reach cover, my host, from his strategic position, neatly killed it.

"Well, there you are!" he observed in that self-satisfied tone a conjuror uses when he has just produced a rabbit from a hat.

Yes, there we were, all of us, including the cobra.

266

But though I could not help smiling to myself at his manner, it struck me as being slightly uncalled for. However, people view things differently.

.   .   .   .   .

That same friend started a pig farm on his estate, of which he had considerable hopes. The young pigs were let loose in the morning to root about in the vlei (a sort of dried morass) and the pigman had trained them to return at mid-day, to the sound of a whistle, for their meal of bran mash or whatever it was. My friend was delighted by this device, which saved so much trouble, and once, when he had some guests staying with him, he said that he had something very clever to show them and would they all come over to the farm with him? So at the proper hour there they were assembled, and my friend, telling them to watch, instructed the pigman to blow a good blast. And sure enough the pigs pricked up their ears and from all over the vlei—some of them were a couple of miles off—began to scamper homewards. But it was broiling hot and they were evidently ravenous, for they ran so fast that no fewer than twenty-seven of them dropped dead from apoplexy.

And this, also, seems to me a rather strange happening, especially to have occurred on the precise day when the training was being demonstrated to an audience.

The Unknown

It was at Taza, which lies seventy-five or eighty miles to the east of Fez, that this adventure began. The friend I was with and myself had expected to be picked up there by the public limousine running to the Algerian frontier, but though they had booked our seats, they had been sold over our heads, and when the car arrived it was already full. In brief, we were absolutely stranded and all we could do was to call on the Colonel in charge of this important French military post and beg for his assistance.

He was a man with the icy eye and the abrupt manner of a rigid martinet, a sort of stage colonel, but he was good enough to lend us an army car to take us to Oujda on the frontier. It was a dilapidated model T Ford, with an utterly exhausted air about it, but as we had to be in Oran by a definite date, it came to us as a godsend.

The Sudanese driver was a gloomy, uncommunicative youth and he, no more than ourselves, had ever been over the road before. Not that it mattered; it was simply a question of keeping straight on. At least, that is what we supposed at the time.

It is, in the main, a desolate tract of country from Fez to Oujda, as if all the rich soil of Morocco were concentrated in the west; but at places the road approaches to the Riff, and as the French were then waging furious war with the tribesmen, there was always the faint, but disagreeable, prospect of being held up by a marauding band. This thought, together with the strong appeal of an untrodden wilderness, kept us from being at all bored.

But just as we were congratulating ourselves on having evaded trouble, trouble began. And with a vengeance! For a start, all four tires got punctured, one after the other, as did several spare tubes we were carrying. In addition, the petrol pipe got blocked up and, if I remember aright, the ignition went wrong. We were able to patch up the last two defects, but we had no means of mending punctures and all we could do was to pump frantically for a few minutes, dash on for a mile or so, and then pump again.

We were due to reach Oujda during daylight, but darkness overtook us while were still far away and then, to add to everything, the lamps failed to act. Now, as I have said, none of us knew the road or, of course, what was on either side of it, so we just had to trust to luck in the pitch blackness of that night. It was not diverting, for every now and then, before we could get our breath, we would find ourselves shooting over alarmingly narrow bridges, which crossed, heaven knows, what hideous ravines and whose white parapets were not more than about two feet high. And if the bridges spanned ravines, for all we could tell the road edged precipices.

By now the driver had lost his stolidity and was in a whimpering condition of fright. The accumulated misfortunes of the day had been too much for him and I believe he would have given up altogether had not my friend, in a menacing voice, kept threatening him every few minutes with the terrible name of the Colonel. It was the one thing which he seemed to fear more than the road, and though he was on the verge of literal collapse before the end, he did manage to keep going. I felt sorry for him.

Well, it was dismal enough in all conscience, but we were getting along and Oujda was drawing nearer every minute, when suddenly, without the faintest hint, I had the sensation of floating through space.

That was the exact, incredible sensation. It must have lasted only a fraction of a second, but I had time to feel not only that catch in the breath which comes from an intimation of disaster, but also that sort of astonished helplessness which a bad skid induces. My friend gave a shout and the driver, by an act of instantaneous decision of which I should have thought him totally incapable, spun the steering wheel round and switched us back on to the road before the hind wheels had left it.

We got out to investigate. For anything we knew we might have been overhanging a cliff. And then peering about us with lit matches, we smiled: a grassy slope at a very sharp angle of about sixty degrees led down on to a harmless-looking field. All the same, if we had gone over, the springs would probably have been broken and quite possibly our necks. And even had we made the descent safely, what would our momentary sensations have been in that darkness shrouding the unknown?

As it was, that split second in which one accepted, in a flash, the prospect of imminent death, coming upon one, like a thief in the night, without sound or warning, was something not readily to be forgotten.

The Monster

One of the strangest and most unaccountable things that ever happened to me, happened many years ago when I was a boy in Scotland.

I was sleeping by myself in a rather distant room of the house in which I was born. It was winter time and I remember waking up about two in the morning and, with a delicious sense of warm comfort, staring out of the window at the snow and at the branch of a tree which, some twenty feet away, was weaving backwards and forwards across my sight. I was wide awake, as wide awake as I am now, and therefore it was with the utmost astonishment that I heard all at once the sound of steady, unhurried footsteps approaching the back of the house. In the profound stillness they were perfectly distinct, but considering that the house stood far away from any other and considering the hour of night, there was something that struck me immediately as rather ominous about their leisurely approach.

I heard them come up to the large door which opened out of the back courtyard and was bolted every evening and then, to my amazement, I heard them crossing the stone of the courtyard itself and pause by the back entrance.

That somebody had gained access to the courtyard was sufficiently startling and could only mean that the custom of years had been forgotten and the door left unbolted. It made me very uneasy, but it was nothing to the shock which followed. For suddenly, to my incredulous terror, I heard the steps inside the house itself. It was unbelievable, but there they were, pat, pat, calm, unruffled, on the flagstones of the lower passage. It was impossible that the house could have been left unlocked, utterly impossible, and yet somebody *had* got in, and it was with a kind of fatal foreknowledge that I presently heard the steps climbing the back staircase.

Naturally every corner of the place was an open book to me and I could follow exactly where they were from moment to moment. They reached the top of the stairs, turned sharp to the left, turned sharp to the left again, descended a few steps, came to the door of the room leading to my room, stopped finally before my own door.

By this time I was sitting up in bed with my eyes glued to the door and with horror in my heart. The handle turned and in the opening stood a creature with the face of a fox, which walked on its hind legs. It was dressed in some sort of way and, would you credit it, wore a top hat, which added to its appearance an indescribably macabre touch. But its face, I repeat, was fox-like and it had a bushy tail. It was, perhaps, bigger than a real fox, but it was vulpine through and through, although I admit that it had no rank odour.

It gazed at me with a fixed rather than a malign expression, but did not speak. I shouted out, "Go away!"—how well I remember the exact words!—and it turned round and went away. I heard its steps follow, in retreat, the precise route they had followed before, unhurried and steady as ever, until at last they died out on the road leading to the woods.

Several explanations have been offered. One is that I was drunk; but I had never so much as tasted alcohol in those days. Another is that it was a dream within a dream and that I was asleep the whole time; well, all I can do is to reiterate, emphatically, that I was wide awake. This may not sound convincing, but if one does not know when one is wide awake, what does one know? Of course, I may, for the first and last time, have been subject to an hallucination, but, if so, it was a remarkably thorough one. Still another explanation is that it was a hoax; but who on earth, even if he were able to disguise himself as a fox, could make his legs *shrink?*

The thing seems inexplicable to me, who have pondered it for over forty years.

.   .   .   .   .

Yes, strange things happen in Scotland. My aunt, now dead, told me that many years ago, perhaps fifty or sixty, when she was staying in an old house in that country—I imagine it was on the Borders, where my family comes from—she had this extraordinary experience. Being of a pious disposition, she had knelt down to pray, with closed eyes, before going to bed, when suddenly and overwhelmingly the room seemed pervaded by a feeling of corruption and evil. She had not heard the slightest sound, but instinctively she opened her eyes and there, reflected in the mirror on her dressing-table, which was lit up by tall candles on either side, she saw a vague figure standing behind her, with its hooked fingers just above her head. It must have stolen into the room with the silence of a cat. Frozen with fear she closed her eyes again and prayed fervently, and presently the sense of evil passed and, looking at the mirror again, she was alone.

Now this, it is quite possible, may have been a practical joke. But why the sinister sensation, unless, without being conscious of it, she really *had* heard a faint sound and that, in turn, had created panic—which, in its turn, is capable of creating anything bad. Or, of course, she may have imagined the whole thing. But who knows what the correct explanation is? After all, people who play practical jokes usually boast about them later.

The Limit

The modern motorist seems to derive a particular gratification from going hell for leather. I must say that I do not altogether share this with him, partly from a sense of self-protection and partly because I like to look at the countryside. No, that sort of recklessness does not excite me to any extent, and the same may be said of flying. The feel of speed is lost when there is nothing to compare it with and while I used to enjoy diving down on to the Atlantic, off Long Island, in an amphibian and then soaring up again, I get very little enjoyment out of conventional land flights.

I have never been in a speed-boat, which I imagine must give one a real thrill, and the only occasions on which I have had much pleasure out of the power of even the fastest ocean liners were, when deep in the bowels of the ship, I have watched the green seas rushing past and felt, like an acute pulse in the ear, the throb of the great engines.

But there is one form of speed which I do always find exhilarating, and that is fast railway travelling. The sense of force and of vast bulk, the complete relaxation of sitting in your corner and staring out on the world as it hurtles by, the sway of the train, the sound of the wheels, all shout to me of a glorious triumph over the inertia of gravity and the smug superiority of the elements.

And from this point of view, the most exciting railway journey I ever made was on the trial trip of the London and North Eastern's streamlined train, "The Silver Jubilee," on September 27, 1935.

Of course, one was attuned to enjoy oneself by the excellent refreshments supplied free by the Company and by the spirit of expectation which inspired everybody, but apart from that, the run really was a unique experience. Never before have I been conscious of such speed, never before have I felt such victorious might.

We attained a pace of one hundred and twelve and a half miles an hour, and though a train in Germany has been timed, I believe, at one hundred and eighteen miles an hour for a short distance, yet ours was nearly a record for the world and a then absolute record for England. An aeroplane, flying low beside us in order to take moving pictures, suggested a race in which we were not being worsted, and this, together with the speed with which the landscape whizzed by—it really did whizz—and the incessant click-click of the wheels spinning over the rail-joints, gave me the sense of travelling even faster than we were.

Crowds had assembled all along the line to see the

silver-coloured train on this, its first public appearance, and the journey was one conquering procession. But whereas the word "procession" suggests, in the ordinary way, something stately and slow, our procession suggested a race against time itself.

It was, indeed, "the limit."

.　　.　　.　　.　　.

I have had it in my mind to describe, as yet another strange happening, my experiences as foreman of a High Court jury. But perhaps they were strange only to me, strange not in a sinister but a fantastic sense, so I will refrain. But I shall never forget the frightful moment when, asked by the Clerk of the Court, whether we found for the Plaintiff or the Defendant, the meaning of the words utterly left me and I gaped speechlessly at him. I do not know how long the silence lasted, but I managed to save myself by mental concentration of an agonizing nature. And then, just as I was feeling better, he shot at me, "Against which Defendant do you find?" Their names had gone with everything else, but I mumbled something which was evidently good enough, for shortly thereafter I was in the street, a free man listening to my own thoughts and not to any well-worn, heavy statement about the propriety of "coming quiet." An ignominious reminiscence, but, after all, who would not have lost his nerve under the frigid stare of the late Mr. Justice Avory!

Queer Spots

WILD FAIR
PIGEON CAVE
PITCH LAKE
DESERTED TOWN

△

It is an easy transition from "Strange Happenings" to "Queer Spots," and I hope the little pictures which follow will be of some interest. I suppose that, by casting one's mind back, one could make a chapter like this many times as lengthy; but I doubt whether vignettes appeal to many people and so, perhaps, it is just as well to be brief. One cannot go far wrong by saying too little, but one can become a fearful bore by saying too much. Next to being facetious, which is unforgivable, to be long-winded is about the worst literary offence.

CHAPTER XIX

Queer Spots

Wild Fair

THE GRACIOUS OUTLINE OF
the Koutoubia dominates the plain about Marrakesh,
and in its rosy calm of eight hundred years, that tower,
in noble solitude, seems to watch over the desert and
the town. You see it afar as you cross the oasis, whose
gardens and pools, whose flowering trees and irrigation
canals, are sweet to the sight after the aridity of the
wilderness. There it stands on the outskirts of the city,
completely harmonious in its great height and austere
design, and utterly untypical of this incoherent, violent
place. Two other Moorish towers of victory were built
at the same time, the Hassan at Rabat and the Giralda
at Seville. I may have seen the Hassan, though I do
not remember, but I have certainly seen the Giralda
and, indeed, have climbed to the top of it. By general
consent, however, the Koutoubia is the most impressive
of the three.

But, as I say, its dignity and its repose are totally alien to the spirit of Marrakesh. For Marrakesh, which is as African as it is Moorish, has a wild, fanatical population and the town itself is made up of twisted streets, palaces, ruined walls, barricaded courtyards, hovels—an intricate, strange town throbbing with a sort of mad vitality.

The pagan rites of the converted Africans are but thinly concealed under the teachings of the Prophet, and the religious brotherhoods with which Marrakesh is honeycombed keep the population in a perpetual state of feverish excitement. Worked up into frenzies and ecstasies during religious festivals, men do not hesitate to cut themselves with knives, to swallow glass or scorpions, to give rein, indeed, to all the inherited instincts of their dark ancestry. But even at ordinary times, when there is no Mohammedan festival to stir the people into special hatred of Unbelievers, one is conscious, even more than in Fez, of explosive material. Looks of distrust and contempt follow one and in the hoarse laughter of the multitude there is a hint of menace.

Truly one feels in Marrakesh as if Africa and Arabia had met together. Both in its appearance and its populace there is something barbaric, and I am not surprised that in the olden days the Jews led a terrified existence in their mellah—a curious warren of a place, full of bolt-holes and sharp corners—and that even to-day they

282

shut themselves up at night within their walled quarter.

But if one wishes really to get at the heart of Marrakesh and to see it in all its extravagance, one must wander through the enormous central square as evening begins to fall and the nightly fair is being held. It is an indescribable sight and leaves on one a most singular impression. Here are jugglers and snake-charmers from Central Africa, story-tellers from Tunisia, holy men from the East, Negro donkey-boys and slaves, grave bearded men from Fez and Casablanca, merchants just arrived with caravans from Mogador, Moorish peasants from the surrounding plains, Jews from the mellah, Algerian dancers, fierce horsemen from the Atlas. They mingle and jostle in a seething, polyglot crowd, forming into groups, breaking away, and the sounds which they emit, broken and raucous, seem but the inevitable counterpart of their unceasing, diverse energy. I have been to all sorts of markets throughout the world, but in sheer fantasy this outmatches every one of them.

From a sky of washed blue the sun beats breathlessly down. The days, even in autumn, are unbearably hot in Marrakesh; but stifling though it be, an evening breeze will soon begin to blow from off the mountains and a coolness to creep into the air. A most blessed coolness which enables one to sleep in comfort.

And as dusk begins to deepen and the afterglow to fire the West, raise your eyes to the range of the Atlas and be rewarded by one of the sights of the world. With the declining sun reflected on the snows, the far-flung, undulating pile takes on an exquisitely ethereal beauty. There are no peaks any more, none at all, no upper outline; only a ridge of violet flame pulsing above the earth.

.   .   .   .   .

One should not visit Marrakesh without driving out the twelve miles to Tameslought, where, in a vast medi-æval castle, which looks as if it were constructed of dried mud, lives a famous Sharif, a descendant of Moham-med and belonging to the family of Mulai Idris, the first Sultan of Morocco. Set in the desert, amid its olive groves, this loop-holed fortress, with storks' nests on every turret and hundreds of pigeons flying around its walls, presents a very striking spectacle. The Sharif's son, with the face of a Moorish aristocrat and the side-locks of a warrior, received us courteously and immedi-ately ordered a banquet in our honour. I have described a Moorish banquet elsewhere in this volume, so will merely say that this one was quite up to expecta-tion. It was two repleted men who returned to Mar-rakesh that afternoon.

Pigeon Cave

On a certain plateau of barren Government land in the Transvaal, where nobody lives and cultivation is impossible, there is a deep cave surrounded by a few scrubby bushes and inhabited by baboons and wild pigeons. As one approaches towards sunset the baboons make off—there is always a sentinel on watch when the animals are there—and coming to the edge and looking down, one might pronounce it, indeed, a hopelessly forlorn and dreary spot. The stony, empty moor stretches away in all directions, and the cave suggests a trap, scooped out by a giant, to catch any unwary traveller crossing his domain.

All the same, it had a great fascination for me, a much greater fascination than had the weird cave I visited near Ipoh in the Malay States, for instead of bats emerging at the fall of dusk, pigeons, large green pigeons, flying swift and sure, converge upon it at that hour. They speed in from all sides, bright arrows out of the dimming sky, to settle for the night on the ledges and parapets of the cave. I dare say that their feeding-grounds may be forty or fifty miles away, but what is that to them? From time immemorial, no doubt, they have been making these daily flights, and perhaps my companion, a local farmer, was the first man to discover their retreat.

And what a discovery it was! We used to trudge the weary miles up from the low ground, carrying guns and cartridges, and then, crouching in the bushes, await the homecoming of the guileless birds. It was about as exciting a sport as I ever recall. A green flash here, a green flash there, in front, behind, fast and furious they came as twilight descended.

Those on the wing hardly seemed to hear the shots, and though the nearer birds may have turned away, the others were not in the least discouraged. I presume that they so little suspected man's presence that nothing short of our actually walking about instead of bending low amid the inadequate cover would have frightened them. The time for shooting was limited, just as the time for catching mackerel in a cove hangs upon the turn of the tide, but the sport was not only superb but certain.

And somehow the utter desolation of the surroundings added to one's enjoyment. One felt so entirely free from interference, so completely isolated. And as it began to darken in earnest, the cave, cut straight into the dolomite, became eerier than ever, as if it housed some deadly animal of the night which would suddenly emerge with a roar and a rush. It looked dank and cold down there, but that did not prevent my companion, who was, himself, as agile as a leopard, from climbing down its precipitous sides to pick up the birds.

And then we would start homewards with our burden, while the sky of Africa, all-glittering with stars, seemed to be reeling round us, and the silence of Africa, a silence apt to be broken by strange cries and chuckles, hemmed us about. There are no such nights as those

286

of Southern Africa; they have an immensity, a calm, as of a sentient spirit, and from the ground arise delicious, mingled odours from that vast carpet of flowers which makes of the veld a botanical wonder.

I shall never see that cave again—I hope nobody ever will and that the pigeons may be left in peace—, but equally I shall never forget it.

Pitch Lake

In the ward of La Brea, a part of Trinidad which looks, surprisingly enough, more dreary than tropical, lies the celebrated Pitch Lake. Walking up from the shore one comes upon it, within a mile of the sea, over the brow of a little hill. And at first glance, it really does resemble a lake of deepest black—a pitch-black lake, let us say—and it is uncanny to see men moving over its surface and tramway lines spanning its breadth.

One associates the idea of pitch with something sticky and soft, but in most places the Pitch Lake is as hard as the asphalt into which it is refined. At first one steps upon it gingerly, despite the evidence of one's eyes, for that shining darkness has treachery written all over it, but when one observes Negro workmen hewing out blocks with pickaxes all fear vanishes.

And yet the "lake" *is* dangerous in certain places. Here and there are what one might term runnels of lighter-coloured pitch, motionless runnels a few feet across. The pitch there has not hardened, never does harden, and if you step on these runnels you will be sucked in slowly, surely, until you are swallowed from sight. A ghastly death!

The very appearance of the lake has given rise to exaggerated rumours about it. A Negro employee assured me that it was four thousand feet deep, but an English oil engineer told me that that was simply not true. Borings, he added, show that the "lake" is a kind of inverted cone, with its apex at the centre, reaching a depth of two hundred and sixty feet. But that would almost seem to me an exaggeration in the opposite direction. For a long time—the "lake" was first worked commercially in 1888—they have been taking out about two hundred thousand tons of pitch a year and, though I am no calculator, I feel that so relatively shallow a deposit would have begun to show signs of giving out by now. And yet the level of the "lake" has sunk relatively little: due probably to the pressure of gas from beneath on this easily melted material, the surface, solid as it looks, fills up imperceptibly in three or four days, however much be removed.

The "lake" is about a hundred and four acres in extent, but only a small portion towards the middle is put to use. Were the world ten times as large as it is, the "lake" could supply its need for asphalt with ease. It is an almost inexhaustible storehouse of wealth and the Trinidad Government derives considerable revenue from royalties paid by the company that leases it.

This company has constructed a plant between the "lake" and the sea, and there the raw product, which contains only forty per cent of bitumen, the remainder being made up of water and clay, is partially refined and packed into barrels. These are then placed, two together, in open cradles and sent by an endless overhead pulley down to the long jetty, where ocean-going ships load them for countries all over the globe.

On three sides the "lake," which lies, for the most part, but a few feet below its banks, is faced by a scraggy jungle. Above the trees there tower the derricks of oil wells, which give, it is obvious, the clue to the "lake's" existence. Trinidad is rich in oil and there can be no doubt that the Pitch Lake is merely an ancient seepage from which the oil has evaporated, leaving its residuum of pitch. It is rather curious to learn, by the way, that there is a similar "lake" almost opposite on the mainland of Venezuela.

There is something at once sombre and bizarre about the Pitch Lake. Its withered unreality suggests a landscape of the moon, while the sizzling bubbles which rise in groups speak of ferment beneath. A faint and not unpleasant odour exhales from it, and pools of rainwater, drawn off by powerful pumps, glisten here and there. The place has an air of death; and yet, for some reason or other, it is the haunt of all manner of

289

birds. What they can find to eat on the Pitch Lake, or why they like to strut about it, are mysteries to me.

Deserted Town

Ninety-two miles south-west of Mandalay, the great city of Pagan, deserted now for over seven hundred years, stretches for twenty miles along the banks of the Irrawady. I know of few more mournful sights. The ancient pagodas which crown the cliff convey a sense of utter loneliness and abandonment, and the thought that behind them, invisible to your gaze, lies an immense dead city powerfully affects the imagination. It is all so still and so majestic, all so full of timelessness, that it fades from view rather as a dream fades from memory.

Now no more than a name and a ruin, Pagan must once have been amongst the most splendid of cities. Nine thousand nine hundred and ninety-nine was the reputed number of its pagodas, and though the vast majority have crumbled to pieces, the dry air of upper Burma has marvellously preserved others. It must be a tragic vista that spreads before one in the deep silence of the wilderness. Undergrowth riots about its streets, they say, creeps over its buildings, gives to its huge remains an air of irretrievable desolation.

It does, indeed, seem unaccountable that man should have raised these innumerable shrines, and some of them, to judge by photographs, incomparably grand—the Temple of Ananda, towering to-day in glorious preservation, would appear to be the grandest of all—only to vanish from the scene. But the reason is known. The city was overrun by a Chinese army in order to avenge the death of ten Chinese nobles who, sent on a mission to the King of Pagan, had been cruelly slain by him. The Chinese did their work and departed for China; the Burmese, thinking the city accursed, never returned. Pagan, in brief, was left to the jungle.

And in time the jungle will overwhelm it completely. Indeed, it might have done so by now but for the efforts of the Indian Government, which looks after some of the finest pagodas. But time is on the side of the jungle: hungry and fertile, it presses upon it from all sides and at long last Pagan will disappear into the forest as, eleven hundred years ago, it arose, like a miracle, from out the forest.

.   .   .   .   .

Thinking of this journey down the Irrawady, has set me thinking of other famous rivers on which I have sailed—on the Zambesi above the Victoria Falls; down the St. Lawrence from Montreal, past Quebec and the island of Anticosti; up the Essequibo through the forests of British Guiana; on the James, with famous old Virginia estates on either shore. And, of course, I have sailed on the summer Hudson and the summer Thames and have known what it is to feel, at one and the same moment, hot, crowded, and glad to be alive.

What a book could be written about rivers, those makers of history, whose names are often the oldest in the land and whose waters are, in very truth, waters of life!

Rare Characters
and Stray Thoughts

▽

*If the chapter before this led from
the chapter before that, this chapter
may, in a similar manner, be said to
lead from both of them. It touches
upon some people who have cut a
figure in the world, though not a
very prominent one, but to a considerable extent it has to do with
people who were, or are, not public
characters at all. And that calls
for anonymity. For while the personality of a celebrity is more or less
common property, the personality
of a private citizen is his own. As
for "stray thoughts," why, a book
has to have a suitable ending.*

CHAPTER XX

Rare Characters and Stray Thoughts

Some of the most remarkable people I have met, men who have definitely impressed and influenced me, had practically no prestige outside of a small circle. They were really great men, but for some reason or other the public knew next to nothing about them. But then reputation, in the wider sense, is not, of necessity, a sign of the highest gifts and fame is bound up as much with chance as with accomplishment.

One such man I have in mind was Arthur Marwood, that friend of Conrad's who died during the War. He had, I think, the deepest and clearest analytic brain I have come in contact with and if he had cared to be a literary critic, instead of a farmer, I believe that he would have revitalized the science of criticism in its more abstract phases. Every week he used to spend an afternoon with Conrad, and to hear those two discussing literature and history was something of which I can never hope to hear the like again. Marwood was a burly Yorkshireman, whose appearance belied the subtlety of his intelligence, but once he started to talk one listened in an enthralled silence. He was very wise and very profound and Conrad found his conversation immensely stimulating.

Mr. Edward Garnett, too, is a critic of rare insight and delicacy and of deserved authority. He is much better known than Marwood ever was, for his has been an active and not a passive life. With his eternally fresh outlook and his uncanny capacity for sensing merit in a hundred directions, he has been unearthing new talent for over forty years. How many writers, from Conrad, Hudson, Galsworthy and D. H. Lawrence, has he not encouraged in their days of obscurity; how many novelists, now famous, has he not helped to mould by his creative criticism! He rediscovered the splendid prose of Doughty and to no literary judgement was Lawrence of Arabia more indebted. Indeed, nobody will ever know all he has done for contemporary letters, but it is not an exaggeration to say that his influence permeates modern English literature.

Under a manner of alarming austerity—he has the coldest eyes I have ever seen—Mr. Garnett is the kindest of men; and if he is contemptuous of the meretricious, he is infinitely helpful where he perceives even a spark of promise. His is a reputation which, with the years, grows in omniscience; and although he remains mysteriously in the background, like a hermit in a cave, yet his name carries extraordinary weight and a word of praise from him is what young writers crave for.

Another remarkable man—one of the most truly remarkable men I have known—was T. E. Hulme, who was killed by a German shell when he was little more than thirty. Had he lived I am convinced that he would have become famous, for his mind had so astonishing an originality, so basic a sanity, and so powerful a drive that he affected everyone as a man of genius. But life being what it is, and despite the fact that he left one posthumous volume behind him full of his special philosophy, I should have supposed that he was now practically forgotten and I was therefore delighted and surprised to learn a few years ago that people are still interested in his personality.

To hear Hulme develop general ideas and abstractions was like studying an elaborate pattern whose inner lines and texture emerge gradually as you gaze. Nothing seemed beyond his range, and as he was also a man of outstanding charm it is not be wondered at that he gathered a salon around him. All sorts of people would attend those weekly gatherings, and though I cannot remember a quarter of them I would mention Gaudier-Brzeska, the sculptor, a brilliant man and, like Hulme, killed in the War, Mr. Ezra Pound, Mr. Ashley Dukes, and Ramiro de Maestu (I fear he has been slain in the Spanish Revolution), a Spaniard after Hulme's own heart and subsequently his country's Ambassador to Argentina. Those evenings are among my most precious memories, but they seem infinitely remote, as, in truth, does everything which happened prior to 1914.

Another frequenter of those parties was A. R. Orage, Editor of "The New Age," who was a friend of Hulme's. Orage was a very engaging, though slightly feline, person, and this, added to the originality of his views and his dialectical ingenuity, made him a force with a large circle of young people. "The New Age" must have seen the earliest writings of many who afterwards became well known and I remember meeting there, amongst others, Mr. Michael Arlen when he was completely obscure. Orage was, perhaps, at his best in the café opposite his office in Chancery Lane, where, surrounded by admirers and disciples, he would expound his ideas with an airy nonchalance which half-concealed his strong convictions. I am glad to notice that a Life of him has recently been published, for he was a striking individual, even if there was about him a certain instability, a certain tendency to be seized by enthusiasms which were apt to die away in time only to lead to new ones. There was, indeed, more than a grain of truth in de Maestu's criticism, "Orage knows the shapes of everything and the weight of nothing," but there was also something noble about his perpetual search for the harmony of existence.

In his last years Orage, after living for a considerable

time in France and the United States, returned to London to edit a revived "New Age." I had not met him since the early days of the War and was looking forward to a reunion, which, for no reason save lethargy, I kept putting off from week to week, when I read that he had died suddenly in the night. It is sad to think that I shall see his friendly smile and yellow tie no more, but if we had met again I dare say we would both have been disappointed. He belonged to a period of my life which, in many respects, is deader than a dodo, and I am not sure that one ought any more to renew lapsed acquaintanceships than one ought to revisit, hopefully, the scenes of one's childhood.

Hulme—to mention him again—was one of the two most invincible arguers I have ever known. The other was J. M. Robertson, a friend of mine for many years and a most able and honourable man. Robertson was something of a celebrity, but I believe that if he had devoted himself completely to the literary and textual criticism of Shakespeare and the Elizabethan drama, which was his great love, instead of spreading his energies over such diverse subjects as politics—he became an Under Secretary of State and a Privy Counsellor—, economics, philosophy and Rationalism, he would have created for himself a more solid reputation. He was a superb logician, and as he possessed, into the bargain, an encyclopædic knowledge, no task of critical detective work or of exegesis would have found him wanting.

Into his one life he had poured the labours of several lives, and while many of his polemical books are already forgotten, he has left behind him an enormous body of scholarship which will survive.

I had a deep affection for both Hulme and Robertson, though they were so diametrically opposed in the processes of their thought that it would never have done to bring them together. There would have been fireworks no doubt, for I cannot imagine either of them giving way, but then there would always have been the possibility of their both turning on me! I did once try the experiment of bringing Conrad and Hulme together: it was not a success.

Another man for whom I had a strong affection was Peter Wenning, the South African artist. He had gained but scanty fame when he died and his work was not so well known as that of two other South African artists I have met, Mr. Gwelo Goodman and Mr. Edward Roworth. But in my opinion it has a distinction all its own. I am informed that nowadays his pictures are much sought after and are, indeed, "priceless." Poor Wenning, who was the gentlest and most sensitive of men, how he would have appreciated a little recognition!

That mingling of gentleness and sensitivity is usually accompanied, both in men and women, by compassion towards others and a modest firmness of character. No wonder that such people are hard to discover, no won-

300

der that once discovered they are never forgotten! Never! They are the only persons with whom one feels even approximately secure.

All the same, it seems to me that the real reasons why one is drawn to people are nearly always more obscure than the ostensible reasons. In other words, it has little to do directly with their qualities, little to do with a community of interests, and almost everything to do with their being, in some way or other, on the same plane as oneself. We have all met men and women to whom we took an instant liking, and we have all met men and women to whom we took an instant and violent dislike. This second appears to me more mysterious and fundamental and is invariably mutual. I have known perhaps a dozen people whom I have loathed at first sight, and as this is very unreasonable I fancy it may have been due to the chance of being on entirely different planes. There is nothing to be done about it, and as hate is a wearing and barren emotion, forgetfulness is wisest.

One of Dickens's minor characters observed on a certain occasion that, "Man without woman would be alone," and though this sentiment is decidedly obvious, yet it is extremely to the point. The society of women is often tantalizing, sometimes torturing, and seldom entirely up to expectation; but without it one would lose that kind of buoyancy which makes life bearable. It is true that when the "come and find me" look fades, recrimination is not far away; but that, presumably, is the swing of the pendulum on which the perilous harmony of romance is founded. In the soft glance and tender word there lie the seeds of indifference, and emotions stretched beyond endurance are apt to be savage in their sudden snapping. It is almost inevitable and often the climax to an internal conflict. For in such friendships, save at their peak, two things may be going on side by side: an outward life which appears to be smooth and an inward life which may be increasingly dissatisfied and critical. A pondered grievance, whether real or imaginary, drowns out pity and justice, and women—men also, indeed—in a revulsion of feeling, want only to strike and strike again. Jealousy gone sour has curious manifestations. It is tragic.

If one were all-wise one could avoid the pitfalls; but then, perhaps, one would miss everything—not alone the heart-break and the cynicism, but the faith, the ecstasy, the feeling of protection. How few people know their own limitations, how few people acknowledge that the fallibility of others is bound up with their own fallibility! Cause and effect govern the most inexplicable actions, but most of us see only the effect. But how can we be sure of tracking to its source the real reason of things? Many a friendship reaches its natural conclusion and the blame one person lays upon another may be due primarily to an inevitable change. But people like to rationalize their moods and

302

to name an outward cause when the real cause may rest within themselves. And that is why even final promises, made unasked for with moving sincerity, ought not to be taken too seriously: none of us can be sure of our own future emotions. Indeed, it is dangerous to trust too completely in anybody: true safety lies only within ourselves.

But existence goes on and from the ashes of disillusionment should arise a finer tolerance and a new understanding. For if there is tragic loss, there is also rebirth, and nobody need ultimately despair. Yes, life goes on with its joys and with its sorrows: one cannot live simply as a moody vegetable.

And as we ask forgiveness from others, so should we grant it—a forgiveness founded on charity, proportion and an underlying humility. It will keep one from the blindness of egocentric brooding and from failing to perceive that the exhaustion of wounded pride finds its instinctive revenge in a desire to turn the tables and inflict insults and suffering. The hidden sadistic streak which lurks in everybody!

But how small and unnecessary it all seems! Why should those capable of tasting the bliss of a fourth-dimensional world have to be haunted by the fear that, around the corner from their fool's paradise, may lie a hell of sordid pain? One imaginative thought, one tactful word, one mutual gesture of tolerance and understanding would avert so many crashes, and kindness, at any rate, ought never to be quenched in the hearts of those who have cared for one another. But it often is, and try as one may to project oneself into the mind of another, bitterness usually remains the arbiter. Devotion both in its beginning and its end is without humour, and in the effort to regain ground one invariably slips further. But then generosity of spirit is rare and self-righteousness is common.

I have ventured to make these few sketchy remarks, dealing with a theme as old as the hills and already the subject of ten thousand books, because it always surprises me to note how many people, including myself, cannot see the wood for the trees. Words like right and wrong, disgraceful and perfect, are used much too glibly; and though one instinctively appreciates and, under all circumstances, readily forgives the processes of one's own logic, one is equally prepared to interpret the processes of another's as mere treachery.

No one, by the way, ever admits to a lack of a sense of humour, just as no one ever admits to snoring, and yet I have met people, and not all of them nonentities, who, even in their normal state, were absolutely devoid of it. It is a painful experience, and all the more so in that such people frequently indulge in a sort of elaphantine capering which they fondly imagine to be intensely humorous. In the other direction, some of the funniest people I have run into, people whose company was a sheer joy, were totally obscure. The most humorous

304

man I ever met, a rough-diamond wit of the purest water, was, I suspect, a bootlegger. And yet after his own fashion he was a genius and one could not listen to him without roaring with laughter. If only people have a sense of humour—and many people, especially women, have it without being themselves humorous—it pardons almost everything. I knew a man once whom I regarded as far from estimable, in fact, as a complete example of a whited sepulchre, with whom nevertheless it was a delight to be. On hearing a doubtful story he would regard the narrator with shocked and incredulous disapproval, but if one watched, one would presently be rewarded by observing him turn his head sideways, while a slow smile, a smile of exquisite comprehension, would well up upon his half-hidden features. He had about as developed a sense of humour as I have seen—he missed no nuance and would repeat a story, as if it were something he could not possibly believe, in a voice of bewildered and pained surprise that was the exact counterpart of his expression, which again would gradually undergo a secret change—, but I would not have trusted him a yard in certain directions.

He was an oddity, all right, and as one looks back some of the people one remembers most clearly were oddities. And by "oddities" I do not mean cranks, who are usually tiresome—though some can be rather entertaining, as, for instance, the man who begged me to head a nudist procession through Hyde Park as a "protest" and the other man who was passionately convinced that if everybody were to eat grass the problem of existence would be solved once and for all—, or lunatics, of whom quite a number seem to be floating about loose, but people who have some quirk of character which makes them stand out in memory. I knew one man, and a man of high ideals, who for some obscure reason had become such a poseur that his real personality had vanished under lairs of sham; I know another, a retired colonel, who was so insistent on enquiring into the why and the wherefore of any views whatsoever you might express that you were driven to thoughts of suicide or murder; I knew still another who had the habit of referring to himself in the third person in terms which, though apparently humble, were really full of self-complacency; I knew a fourth, a steward in an American liner, who, on asking in the friendly American fashion what my profession was and learning that it was that of a writer, remarked judicially, "I thought you were something like that: I saw you reading a book at breakfast." (But perhaps he was not an oddity, perhaps he was only a realist); I knew a fifth who, however meticulously one worded one's business letters to him—and one *did* make them meticulously clear—had a perfect mania for reading into them thoughts which had never so much as entered one's head; and I knew a sixth, a schoolmaster of mine, who, when I returned as an old boy, remarked beamingly, as doubtless he remarked to other old boys, "I've forgotten your name and I don't recall your face, but I know who you are"—an observation which has always suggested to me occult powers of a high order. But enough: such a list could be prolonged for pages, and for all I know some one is now making a similar one and putting me into it.

Ordinary friendship is largely a question of propinquity and by and large it is hopeless to try to keep up friendships by correspondence alone. Friends grow away from one another, as lovers grow cold, and it is melancholy to reflect how many friends one makes, how many potential friends one meets, who become, in time, no more than fading, pleasant memories. Old friendships, I agree, do not fall within these rules, but then they only develop into old friendships through many reunions. I am thinking of some of my old friends as I write and I know that if I were not to meet them again for years there would be no vestige of change. But the man is lucky who can count a handful of such friends and, anyhow, time keeps winnowing their number.

A dim procession of people I have known passes before me: wise people and foolish; good people and bad; complex people and simple; exciting people and dull. Such hundreds, perhaps thousands, of individualities and types that the more one thinks of them, the more dazed one grows in contemplation of human beings. Everywhere the same problems in their myriad disguises, the same triumphs, the same defeats, the same

striving after unattainable happiness. If only one had
something to hold on to, something indestructible! But
that is equivalent to asking for the moon.

Somewhere tucked away in a tin box there lies the
manuscript of my reminiscences of childhood, which
were written at Helouan, near Cairo, in 1913. They
are, of course, of little interest to anybody but myself,
but glancing through them again recently, they did
vividly recall the thrilling, secret atmosphere in which
I passed my earliest years. From the smell of haylofts
to the tang of winter mornings, from the hush of pine
woods to the cool prattle of mountain burns flowing between banks of bracken, everything had an inner significance. One's daily life was shared with other children,
but one had an incommunicable life of one's own which
one neither would, nor could, have shared with anyone.

No doubt this is a common experience, for there is a
dawn of magic in all our hearts, but I still feel an envy
to think how once the most ordinary book or the most
usual scene could create a realistic symbolism which
stirred me more than does the finest emanation of man's
brain to-day. This, I suppose, is only to say what
Wordsworth said in poetry; but, nevertheless, as it
comes to all of us as a new wonder and leaves in all of
us a sort of pang, it is, perhaps, worth saying again. We
shed as we take on, and I would give all the gains of
adult experience for that lost power to read into the
world what I wanted to find there. Now I am con-

stantly finding in the world what I do not want to; then I had a wizard's, which is a child's, gift to transmute everything into gold.

And yet I do not want my youth over again—which does not imply that I do not often instinctively wish to be young or do not occasionally have the disturbing thought, "I am older at this very moment than I have ever been before"—, for so far as I can see, one is hardly justified in being an optimist about life. (All the same, I am planning about six new books!) Its enticement is a nacreous shell covering the cruel indifference of nature and the crueller faithlessness of humanity and our bodies are miserable tenements for immortal dreams. And then, too, the earth grows cloudier with unrest from day to day. We are on the slipping verge of a new experiment in civilization and I cannot honestly say that I am anxious to witness the upshot. I suppose it will have its value, just as other people will arise as interesting and curious as any I have known, but that is another matter. Each generation must face its own troubles and study its own personalities. I am content—well, "content" is not the precise word, shall I say "resigned"?—to have lived a fairly full life, travelled a good deal and met a number of remarkable persons. What more could one reasonably ask of existence?